What People S

"Carolyn Bartlett's knowled   f
short-cut in getting to know thei   nt.
themselves differently in therapy,   t u
approach works best. I thoroughly   yea   ... ... Enneagram from
this different and refreshing point   iew."
   – Elizabeth Wagele, co-auth   of The Enneagram Made Easy, Are You
My Type, Am I Yours?; author, T   nneagram of Parenting, The Beethoven
Enneagram

"The line between spirituality   therapy blurs at a certain depth. Carolyn Bartlett reaches that depth as   ses the Enneagram and draws on her
years of experience. She reveals t   ruggle of each Enneagram style and,
most importantly, how each style   s within it. She is realistic about the
intensity of the struggle, but I fin   t of hope in her work."
   – Richard Rohr, author of   vering the Enneagram, Experiencing
the Enneagram

"The Enneagram Field Gu   is compelling and comprehensive. It
builds an important bridge betwee   Enneagram and mainstream psychology. Carolyn Bartlett offers valuab   sights about personality type from the
therapy client's perspective, gleane   m interviews and years of therapeutic
experience. This book is for anyone   ested in personal growth, as well as for
therapists who want to better und   nd the inner world of their clients."
   – Andrea Isaacs, Co-founder   editor, Enneagram Monthly; creator
of EnneaMotion and Physical I   igence Trainings

"The Enneagram is most effe   when it is grounded in disciplined
observation, the kind that trained t   pists do well. Carolyn Bartlett is such
a therapist and this book bristles w   pecific, in-depth examples of how Enneagram styles play out in the fles   rtlett takes the painful revelations of
real people in therapy and illustra   ow they can be helped by therapists
who understand the Enneagram. R   t that she is, she also tells us what will
not work. If you are a therapist or   us student of the Enneagram, here is
much gold to mine."
   – Clarence Thomson, autho   Parables and the Enneagram; editor,
Enneagram Applications, The Elec   Enneagram

"Carolyn Bartlett has provided   ith a very thorough and easy-to-read
resource guide for understanding   ine Enneagram types in a new and
refreshing way. I use the Enneagra   my consulting practice and, while I
am not a therapist, I still found th   formation invaluable in understanding what makes my clients tick an   y. The information is presented in a
way that allows me to understand   h Enneagram style at a deeper level

and has helped me to better work with my clients. The usual result is they become better managers, leaders and human beings. Carolyn's contribution is invaluable."
 – Dennis Tallon, management consultant and OD practitioner, Quantum Consultants, Denver, Colorado

"These chapters offer excellent advice and delicious examples of appropriate psychotherapy for the nine types. This level of work is most helpful for spiritual practice. Those of us pursuing spiritual truth and freedom, whatever our path or tradition, can easily be distracted by the insistent demands, hurts, needs, and projections of ego. When enough of these are relaxed and ameliorated, we more easily see that which is beyond 'me' and 'mine.'"
 – Ven. Santikaro Bhikkhu, Buddhist Monk

"The Enneagram Field Guide is the definitive guide for any therapist who wants an in-depth understanding of their clients. With wisdom and compassion, it clearly illuminates the path of growth for all nine types including insightful suggestions for therapy."
 – Julie Foster, MA, Psychotherapist and Enneagram Teacher

"Many clients have come to me reporting that they've been to therapists who were supportive and competent, but "nothing changed," whereas after a few of our coaching sessions they have begun to experience the kind of breakthroughs they'd been looking for. Am I better than a good therapist? No. Do I have a magic wand? Yes. It's the Enneagram, and my therapist colleagues who are Enneagram-knowledgeable report the same positive results that I find in coaching.

Carolyn Bartlett draws from her counseling background and from interviews with people of all nine styles to show brilliantly and clearly how therapists who know the Enneagram can enhance their diagnostic acuity, develop the best treatment plans and use the skills they already have to their best advantage."
 – Mary Bast, co-author, *Out of the Box: Coaching with the Enneagram*

"The Enneagram Field Guide represents a breakthrough effort to bring the Enneagram understandings into counseling and therapy. Carolyn provides many insights in what does work synthesizes and systematically reviews therapy strategy with each of the Enneagram types. She provides clarity, compassion and thoughtfulness in her writing. All of us in the fields of counseling, ranging from executive coaching to spiritual direction, will find this guide of great and enduring benefit. It is a pleasure to recommend it."
 – David Daniels, M.D., Clinical Professor, Department of Psychiatry and Behavioral Sciences, Stanford Medical School

The Enneagram Field Guide

Notes on Using
the Enneagram in
Counseling, Therapy
and Personal Growth

Carolyn Bartlett

Nine Gates Publishing
Fort Collins, Colorado

Published By
Nine Gates Publishing
P. O. BOX 343
Fort Collins, CO 80522
(970) 484-7868
http://www.insightforchange.com

Cover design by Courtenay Kelley
Printed in the United States of America

Previous Publisher and ISBN: The Enneagram Consortium 1-932601-01-5

Publisher's Cataloging-in-Publication
(Provided by Quality Books, Inc.)

   Bartlett, Carolyn, 1950-
      The enneagram field guide : notes on using the enneagram in counseling,
      therapy and personal growth / Carolyn Bartlett.
      p. cm.
      Includes bibliographical references and index.
      LCCN 2007926331
      ISBN-13: 978-0-9790125-4-9
      ISBN-10: 0-9790125-4-6
      1. Enneagram.   I. Title.

   BF698.35.E54B38 2007
   155.2'6
                    QBI07-600140

                                                      2007926331

*For my husband, John Reynolds, who sees the best in everyone,
including me.
And for the dreamers of Cave - Gladys and Leslie.*

Acknowledgements

I want to thank each person who volunteered their time to fill out questionnaires and answer personal questions about their therapy. This is the heart and soul of my book. Somehow these volunteers always gave what was needed at the time. So many people contributed to the book, either by telling their stories, giving honest feedback or critically reading chapters from the perspective of their type. The final product is a patchwork quilt created by a community.

I especially want to thank Tom Condon for his generosity, for sharing his expertise with the Enneagram and therapy as well as with prose. The book is much better as a result of his patient and kind editorial assistance.

I'm grateful to John and Lisa Zimmerman who introduced me to the Enneagram and to Julie Foster. Julie has been my teacher, mentor and clinical supervisor. Gladys Wolff, John Reynolds and Leslie Dwyer were colleagues and consultants in learning to apply the Enneagram to different psychotherapy models. They sent me their clients to interview and offered feedback, encouragement and ideas. Julie Foster was always available to deepen my understanding of the underlying motivation for each Enneagram style as well as their childhood experience, connecting points and spiritual aspects. She also helped describe the healthy manifestation of each style.

I appreciate the other midwives of this project who read, edited, advised, and provided insight: Gladys Wolff reviewed each chapter. Those who provided selected editorial review are: Liz Wolk, Dorsey Moore, Bruce Hall, Stephen Hatch, Ven. Santikaro Bhikkhu, Ken Hoole, Bonnie Shetler, Julie Foster, John Reynolds, Patti Wolff, Dana Cain, Leslie Dwyer, and Cherrie Thornton.

Other people who supported the work in some critical way are: Nancy Hansford, Karl Kopp, Judith Searle, Dennis Tallon, Jenny McKillop, Deb Wescott, Marc Husson, Martha and Richard Bartlett, Corrina Bartlett and Evan Deck.

Enneagram Monthly published articles and chapters allowing me to stay connected with Enneagram enthusiasts. The IEA and the Narrative Teachers Association also provided opportunities to share what I was learning and to learn more myself. Thanks also to Marian Woodman for giving me permission to quote passages from Addiction to Perfection.

Contents

vi

Introductio

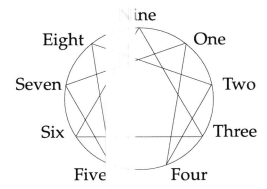

On Christmas Eve 1991 c   ew neighbors invited my husband and me to their home for a ho   celebration and, during the course of the evening, introduced u: he Enneagram. We had never met them, but my daughter had b   babysitting their children, and they seemed to have a lot of insigl   o her for having known her such a short time. By the end of t   vening they were hinting at our Enneagram styles and sent u   me with Helen Palmer's book *The Enneagram*.

Never a fan of typing s)   ns, I was initially doubtful but still intrigued by my neighbors' i   hts. I eventually agreed with their "typing" of me as well as of n   sband and daughter, but only after I investigated it on my own.   ite my distaste for labeling people I found the Enneagram's desc   on of personality styles to be subtle, complex and useful.

My husband John and I l   n to study the system in depth with Julie Foster, Helen Palmer,   David Daniels. We also took an occasional workshop from ot   eachers and created our own study groups. The more I learned   it the Enneagram, the more I was amazed by its diagnostic a   It was also democratic; despite differing worldviews and n   ations, each personality style was portrayed as equally gifted c   ually troubled.

John and I first applied t   nneagram to our personal relation-ships and found it so useful v   entually applied it to our work. We are both psychotherapists and we found right away that the system deepened our understanding of our clients and showed us our own counter-transference. We also found that it greatly enhanced the other theoretical models that we used in treatment. Eventually we began to teach it to our therapist consultation group.

Although each client has unique needs, the Enneagram suggests a general direction for treatment that is influenced by the parameters of type. The more we applied the system to our work the more we noticed that what was effective with some personality styles didn't work as well with others. Our consultation group helped us connect the Enneagram with different approaches to psychotherapy. John and I then decided to share what we had learned with other therapists in our public seminars.

In August 1999, John and I led a workshop at the International Enneagram Association conference in Toronto. The audience was composed of psychotherapists who were applying the Enneagram in their work. To prepare for the workshop we interviewed individuals who knew their Enneagram style and had been through counseling or therapy. We wanted to know what they thought had worked for them from the perspective of type. We deliberately chose people who were not our clients and interviewed them at length. At the workshop in Toronto we presented our results. The therapists were excited to learn what clients had to say and the idea to write this book was born.

At this point John handed further development of the project over to me and I continued to gather information about people's experiences with counseling and therapy. I ran an ad in the *Enneagram Monthly* magazine as well as other venues. My assessment tools included a questionnaire by mail or e-mail followed by more detailed questions in selected interviews (see appendix).

Several people of each Enneagram style gave me especially generous in-depth interviews. In addition, I spoke with friends, colleagues, and people I met at conferences, as well as those who were in our workshops. I asked questions like: "What do you wish psycho-therapists and counselors understood about your type?" Or I would define the most difficult part of doing therapy with a given Enneagram style and then ask representatives of that style: "What do you sug-gest?"

The people who shared their personal experience in these con-versations and interviews provided most of the material in this book. I learned from them and applied their advice in my own work. My hope is that this book will help other practitioners who want to skillfully apply the Enneagram.

The Enneagram and I   hotherapy

The Enneagram is not   odel of therapy itself, but can be applied to any treatment app   h. It exists on the boundary between secular and spiritual psych   y. Spiritual psychology holds that each human being has a sacre   t to offer, but as we react defensively to the pain of human experier   our gift is obscured. An individual's defense can resemble their   ut it is actually a protective mask, often referred to as a "persor   'false self," "fixation" or a "trance." People labeled co-dependen   example, are usually gifted at being compassionate; however, the   y warp the capacity to disguise and protect their early wounds. E   entifying a client's type of false self, a therapist can understand th   ture of their underlying wound and see what the client really wa   n its place.

Learning the Enneagra   ll help you in a myriad of ways. It will enhance your diagnosti   ity and help you quickly recognize people's different motivatic   coping strategies and relationship patterns. If you are a therapis   ounselor it will guide you to the best treatment plans for a give   nt and suggest how to time and sequence your interventior   he beginning of therapy involves joining with and understand   he client's worldview as accurately as possible. The Enneagram   help you establish rapport and build trust with greater speed anc   cision. Once the client feels under- stood and trusts the therap   he work of change can effectively begin.

It is not easy to ask for   . Clients come to therapy for many reasons but usually an exte   life change or internal feelings are causing them incongruence   pain. Sometimes this cause is an obvious event – divorce, dea   ob loss; other times clients arrive in therapy troubled by interna   ings like depression or free-floating anxiety. It is unusual for hu   beings to challenge their defensive patterns as long as the patter   e effective and most people usually have to be very uncomfortab   fore they call a therapist. Experienc- ing emotions that overwheli   eir defenses, they hope therapy can help. Their vulnerable self is   lable to the therapeutic relationship, ready to change.

The self-exposure requ   by psychotherapy, however, is not entirely comfortable. Clients   ry about how the therapist sees them as well as what they may dis   er about themselves. There is almost always a tension between tr   to drop the mask while still staying protected. Then there is the   tion of trust: Can the client depend on the therapist to provide real help? How much self-revelation is safe? Clients at this stage may question whether change is even possible.

In fact, sitting down in a therapist's office often heightens a client's defenses and they may resist the situation with the very patterns they are there to change. Good therapists recognize that these defenses are at play in the circumstance and that clients will need them for protection until they feel safe.

When a therapist sees how a client's defense works, it gives them an edge. The Enneagram helps by precisely identifying the specific defense mechanism that supports the neurotic habit – akin to an addiction – of each style. This unconscious automatic reaction keeps the client from feeling exposed, even at the cost of limiting themselves further.

Psychotherapeutic process usually begins with the therapist affirming the client's essential self while examining the negative impact of their defensive style. Later the therapist has to shift from playing a solely supportive role and begin to encourage the client to take responsibility for what they can change. This may entail confronting them with the fact that they now inflict on others what was done to them in the past; that what once worked as a survival tool now causes suffering. A therapist needs to skillfully gauge a client's readiness to tolerate such insights. Otherwise the client might feel shamed, setting the therapy back.

The Enneagram can smooth this sometimes difficult transition, providing therapists with a road map they can pass along to their clients. Some clients find that learning about their Enneagram style helps them see through their behavior to underlying patterns and appreciate their defenses in a compassionate light. By learning about the common experience of other people with the same Enneagram style, clients realize they are not alone or unique in their difficulties. They also recognize there are reliable ways to transform the suffering created by their personality defenses. From this perspective change can seem survivable and even exciting.

By studying the Enneagram, clients can better understand their own motives and begin to recognize that their personality pattern is not who they are. Since it is impossible to simultaneously observe your story and live it, this strengthens the client's ability to be more objective about themselves. They learn to observe their defenses rather than act them out. The Enneagram can further encourage clients by providing accounts of others like them who have successfully changed.

Certainly not all client: l be interested in the Enneagram nor is that necessary for a ther t to still make good use of it. Some clients do, however, find it able and the common language and perspective the system offe n enhance the therapy partnership. Many good books, worksho nd videos are available and some are listed in the bibliography.

As I mentioned, the E gram is also a spiritual psychology offering a larger transpersc framework for clients to understand their lives. Something like i d-life crisis might lead a client to see how they have identifed wi nask or role in a general way. At such times their whole rationale iving can start to come apart. Major losses can also motivate cl to deeply question their usual approach to life. From there t may unearth feelings of pain, loneliness and despair – whatevei r defenses have protected them from.

A therapist who unde ids how to use the Enneagram in a spiritual way can help clie cognize their deeper gifts and their essential nature. The therap might also communicate to the client that their defensive person sn't need to immediately be fixed or replaced. Learning to live v fewer defenses, in a way that allows the clients to express their c tial qualities and gifts, is sometimes a better goal. Learning to en the void that opens from the collapse of old defenses is its own g d supports the client's spiritual and psychological transformati

What Does and Does Not Work

The people I intervie from each Enneagram style consistently revealed patterns of cess and failure. Each group shared stories of well-meaning the sts who colluded with their defenses and missed opportunities ffectively intervene. These relationships were safe, but produc o change. Other therapists failed in a more provocative way by c enging their client's story before the client felt understood, caus he client to feel more defensive.

Each group reported s ar patterns of ineffective counseling for their style, usually becai ie therapists either argued with their client's worldview or inapp iately merged with it. Some examples included: fearful Sixes havi ieir worst-case scenarios opposed by a therapist who just met th self-critical Ones being told immediately that they are not that ; therapists setting goals for passive Nine clients and seductive o clients becoming personal friends with the therapist. If there s do not effectively negotiate these dynamics, meaningful char s unlikely.

If the psychotherapist is able to create an environment in which the client feels understood, and believes that the therapist has something to offer, then the opportunity for deeper work emerges. In each chapter I've included stories about how treatment succeeded or failed. Several individuals of each Enneagram style generously read a rough draft of their style's chapter and gave me feedback. I kept only what was most true to their experience and eliminated what they did not relate to. This allowed me to refine the content further, to present a more general picture of what people with each style would want therapists to understand. Of course therapists may see a direction for treatment that conflicts with what the client believes is best, but these guidelines should still be helpful.

One interesting finding was that it did not matter if the therapist or client knew the Enneagram at the time of therapy. The therapists described as most helpful still intervened in ways that addressed the dilemmas of the client's Enneagram style. This both reinforces the validity of the Enneagram and affirms that good therapists intuitively provide treatments that match their clients' needs. However, retrospective reports of negative experiences were also consistent by type and in those cases the Enneagram's insights might have improved the outcome.

Transference and Counter-transference

Treatment failures often seemed related to therapists failing to recognize transference – what the client projects onto the therapist – and counter-transference – what the therapist projects onto the client. Learning to use the Enneagram skillfully often helps the therapist identify his or her own bias – positive or negative – and recognize its impact on treatment. For example, if a Two therapist wants to take milk and cookies to a client's children or a Three therapist gets attached to producing results for a managed care company, they might realize they are caught in counter-transference.

The Enneagram offers an excellent framework to precisely interpret and transcend counter-transference. Typical patterns are described in each chapter. Appendix One also offers additional comments from therapists on the counter-transferential reactions of their style.

Nature Versus Nurture

The question of nature versus nurture – whether a personality style is innate or created by a child's parenting and early environment

– comes up often in Enneaς literature. Some authors have described specific family dy ics as the etiology of someone's Enneagram style. This argu t is especially seductive when you work with the stories and erns of your clients and listen to personal histories that seem cause" their style-specific defenses. However, all of this informa is reported tautologically – from the biased perspective of the sty

Infants and young chilc already seem to exhibit the tendencies of a character style.* W her the cause is nature or nurture, seeing the world through th spective of type provides a sense of security. It helps a child ma ense of overwhelming amounts of information by unconscious ecting what fits with what he or she already knows. Family and c re symbiotically match and respond to the child's efforts, provic a feedback loop that reinforces the child's budding assumptio out the nature of existence. In a family with nine children, ea ith a different Enneagram style, each child would find sufficient ence to confirm their bias. Parents often blame themselves for " ing" their child to "suffer" a particular Enneagram style, but I th its ultimate origins are a mystery.

Nevertheless family an lture provide the child's formative sense of safety, which influ s the degree to which personality defenses are created and carr nto the future. How strongly we feel we need protection is determ d by our basic sense of safety or lack of the same. This is usually r influenced by our early family life, environment and culture. Th rly milieu is often referred to as the "holding" environment. As rapists we are working with the holding environments our cl once knew and their responses to it according to type.

Psychological System nd the Enneagram

Most psychotherapists taught to identify and work with pathology models that incl erms like "major depression" and "psychosis." Teachings tha phasize psychiatric diagnosis are sometimes referred to as a "r cal model." There is a continuum in assessment and treatment m s from those that focus on pathology

*Arguing for the side of nature, C)aniels reports on this in an article called "Nature and Nurture: on Acquiring a Type" (I 1. which is reprinted in *Enneagram Applications*, *Volume One*, edited by Clarence Thomp; d Thomas Condon). He applies information from longitudinal studies of early childhoc idd "Nine Categories of Temperament" to the language of the Enneagram. The work prences is "Temperament and Development," by Dr. Alexander Thomas and Stella Chess York: Brunner/Mazel, 1977). This study indicates nature prevails, as the children observe t to have their personality styles from birth. It also validates the Enneagram because the r pes parallel the system.

to those that frame most behavior as ordinary. Many schools with a humanistic bent resist labeling because of its negative impact, but minimizing an appropriate psychiatric diagnosis can also lead to treatment failure.

People with both humanistic and medical models have been recently developing psychological applications for the Enneagram. While the roots of the Enneagram are obscure and possibly ancient, its history in the context of therapy begins very recently. Claudio Naranjo is a psychiatrist, Gestalt therapist and author from whom many leading teachers in the USA first learned the system in the 1970s. He cross-referenced Enneagram character styles with other typing systems, including the *Diagnostic and Statistical Manual of Mental Disorders*, the most common source of psychiatric diagnoses. Although he spoke in psychiatric language, Naranjo's efforts failed to penetrate professional mental health circles. Instead, the Enneagram became popular in Catholic and Christian networks before eventually emerging into the popular culture. Perhaps this history explains why the system is often presented in humanistic terms. However, efforts to use the system to diagnosis pathology and predict potential are still popular.

The Enneagram identifies character tendencies with great accuracy, which makes it tempting to use it to label and predict. However, if it ultimately becomes another system for labeling pathology, its potential as a transpersonal resource will be lost. Unlike the DSM, the Enneagram presents a fluid continuum for understanding personality patterns including high functioning expressions as well as spiritual potentials and capacities.

Certainly some clients present unhealthy behavior patterns and it is important to start by meeting clients where they are. However, many therapists say that their most skillful work happens when they maintain a "beginner's mind" – being open to their client's potential for change and unattached to a therapeutic outcome. There is always the possibility that the client could grow beyond perceived diagnoses and most therapists have been pleasantly surprised by the hidden strengths of clients who first appeared to be blindly abusive or afflicted. In a similar way, estranged families sometimes reconcile following unexpected events. In addition, individuals and families who initially seem ideal may later reveal harmful secrets and shadows. Any premature clinical expectations based on first impressions can subtly render the psychotherapist ineffective at a time when the client most needs help.

Typing in Practice

To help our clients det[...]ne their Enneagram style we recommend that they take the tes[...] the book *The Essential Enneagram* by David Daniels, M.D. and V[...]ia Price, Ph.D. This test introduces them to the system and help[...]m narrow their probable Enneagram style from nine choices dow[...]hree. After testing we then try to help the client discover which st[...]hey most identify with.

Using a test avoids spe[...]g clinical time asking questions. For clients who are interested ii[...]Enneagram, the process of exploration alone is beneficial, evei[...]akes a while to decide which style is home. For therapists using t[...]nneagram, it is nice to know a client's core style if possible. But, id[...]ying the client's prevalent patterns is useful anyway, even if thei[...]cise style remains unclear.

Some existing diagnos[...]onditions can complicate typing as they seem to have their ow1[...]neagram style. We have noticed, for instance, that Post Traumat[...]:ess Disorder can make people seem like fearful Sixes even wh[...]iey aren't. Trauma often leaves its victims attempting to prote[...]emselves by anticipating worst-case scenarios with hyper vigila1[...]nd scanning, questioning perceived reality and mistrusting aut[...]y. All of these are characteristics of Sixes and it is easy and ten[...]ig to make a premature Enneagram diagnosis based on these qu[...]es. Other PTSD symptoms include a tendency to numb or intelle[...]lize emotions – characteristic qualities of Fives. PTSD also ca[...]its victims to be literal and reduce complex situations into bla[...]id white judgments – similar to the way Ones manage informat[...]Various other medical or personality disorders as well as cultur[...]ntexts can also obscure someone's type.

Because the Enneagra1[...]is become popular through human potential and spiritual vei[...]traditional psychotherapists have been slow to recognize its[...]e. Presently there are a number of researchers in psychology[...]are applying scientific methods to prove the validity of the sy[...]. But, it already has a life of its own outside the culture of psych[...]y. As more and more people find the Enneagram's wisdom benef[...]psychotherapists who know how to apply the system skillfully[...]be in greater demand. By offering therapists insights from the[...]it's point of view, this book is meant to speed your application o[...]s powerful system.

Chapter Organization

The material is organized for quick reference to provide ideas for therapists and counselors using the Enneagram in their practice. Each chapter addresses the following for each character style:

Introduction

Each chapter begins with a list of ways that a particular Enneagram style presents in therapy. This is followed by brief introductory comments about the style, including its healthy and unhealthy qualities and usual habits of attention. Also included are a few observations about how the style intersects with the larger culture. Since the majority of people whose stories are in this book are American, that is the bias.

Childhood Experience and Adult Defenses

Groups of people with the same Enneagram style often describe their childhood experience in similar ways. Each chapter contains a brief composite of the most common themes. This is followed by a description of the style's typical defense mechanism as it arises from childhood wounds and family pressures. Although the defense mechanism I describe is especially pertinent to the "false-self" of the style, an individual may employ a variety of other defenses as well.

Enneagram Styles in Therapy

At the heart of this book are psychotherapy experiences reported from the perspective of the client with a focus on what helped them change. Each chapter offers observations about: What brings clients of that particular Enneagram style to therapy, what does not work in therapy, and typical patterns of transference and counter-transference.

Representatives of each Enneagram personality style reported positive, life-changing psychotherapy experiences and each chapter provides first-hand accounts of what worked for them in therapy. Not surprisingly, specific therapy techniques and approaches were mentioned as both helpful and not by people with the same type. For example, some Fours said that Gestalt Therapy was effective while others said it was not. This is a reminder that techniques and strategies are only useful in the context of a healing relationship. In addition, the interventions and methods mentioned in each chapter aren't exclusively beneficial for the Enneagram style discussed. They could certainly work with other styles.

Connecting Points

The Enneagram is far ... e fluid and multi-dimensional than it first appears and the subtle ... ations in how individuals experience their personality style are ... plex and interesting. There are, for instance, points of connec ... that allow people with one style to experience life through tw ... her Enneagram numbers. Therapists who begin to use the sys ... will notice how their clients behave differently when influence ... these other aspects of self. Descriptions of relevant connectin ... ints and some of the uses a therapist can make of them are inclu ... in each chapter.

Dreams

Dreams are an invalua ... resource in therapy, since the unconscious always seems to spe ... ts truth, however obscurely. Dreams also can provide another w ... understand the internal landscape of an Enneagram style. Each ... ter includes a sample dream selected to illustrate themes comm ... that style.

Good Enough Therapy

The psychoanalyst [... Winnicott coined the term "good enough" to describe a mat ... l relationship that provides the basic safety, love, mirroring and ... tainment needed by the developing child. In analytic literature ... otion has been applied as a template for the basic elements of e ... ive therapy. Each chapter ends with some summary comment: ... ut what constitutes "good enough" therapy for that Enneagra ... le.

Ones

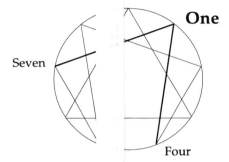

Presentation in Ther[

- One clients can be se   tical and self-deprecating
- They tend to avoid o   lyze emotions; may be workaholic
- They may be depres[r have relationship problems
- Can be prone to con   ive behaviors, anxiety disorders or
obsessive-intrusive "bad" t   hts (ego-dystonia)
- Their personal stori   ay center on resentment for being
overlooked or comparing tl   elves to others
- Ones can be overly fe   d truthful; they can deny their pain
by comparing it to somethi[orse
- In couples therapy, [may act self-righteous and portray
their partner as the identifi[tient
- Ones may abuse sub[es in an effort to relax or quiet their
over-active super-ego. Sub   es also allow Ones to express the
shadow side of being so m[sometimes referred to as "trap door
behavior."

Healthy Ones have hu[tarian natures. They want to do their
best, give of themselves and   e the world better for everyone. They
also allow themselves to ha   y and pleasure, accepting their own
and others' flaws with com   ion and humor.
When caught in their   ealthy pattern, Ones are obsessive
about what seems wrong   how it should be corrected. They
become angry; critical of th   lves and others and unable to let in

any perspective other than the one they think is right. They can see themselves as alternately bad and good in a black and white world. The usual One attention style fixes on ethics, fairness and "work before pleasure." They notice what needs improving and feel compelled to act on this perception.

Ones often express their moral intensity through political action. Ideologically, they fall on either end of the political spectrum; however, the prevailing power of the religious right is a cultural embodiment of One-flavored righteousness.

Ones often get a double message in American culture. Calvinism was influential in the founding of America and this mentality supports the Ones' critical moralistic assumptions. At the same time, Americans value personal freedom, sometimes to a hedonistic degree. From this angle, Ones get the message that their moralism is tiresome.

Childhood Experiences and Adult Defenses

Ones have the inherent gift of fully enjoying the beauty and perfection of the world exactly as it is. They also naturally notice what could be better and want to use their talents to help.

As children, however, Ones' basic trust in their own value is interrupted. This early wounding comes from feeling caught off-guard by criticism, which is humiliating and feels like a blow to the gut: "I grew up in a critical family and being criticized made me feel like I was too bad to exist – I wanted to disappear to avoid that feeling." Many Ones remember being criticized for responding spontaneously to pleasure and sensation. They began to distrust their emotions and instincts and rely on their minds instead to discern the rules of survival.

To avoid criticism, a One child learns to vigilantly internalize standards of rightness and goodness. A formidable super-ego develops, referred to as the "inner critic" in Enneagram circles. Ones often were "good" little boys and girls who overachieved in school or in their community. Although some remember being rebellious, they were still driven by trying to be good and right according to internalized standards. Genograms, or family maps, of Ones suggest that many played "over-functioning" roles as children.

In the service of being good, Ones disown their anger. They then guard against being consciously aware of it with the defense mechanism of reaction formation – directing their overt behavior or attitudes into precisely the opposite direction of their underlying, unac-

ceptable impulses. This de   protects the One from recognizing
their anger or other feelir   ncongruent with their perfectionist
ideals. So a One could work   n he wants to play or compensate for
feeling angry by acting esp   ly pleasant.
A female One offered   xample: "I went to get a biopsy for a
suspicious lump. The surg   said she wouldn't be able to do the
biopsy in the office as pl   d, but would need to schedule the
hospital and anesthesia, a   ould do it when she returned from
vacation in two weeks. Fe   ; strangely detached from my own
reactions, I redirected the   versation into small talk about her
vacation. My friends told m   t she should have given me a referral
to another surgeon, but I ass   them I was fine with waiting–which
I believed until a few days   r when I was listening to a weather
report on the radio. It menti   disastrous weather in the city where
she was vacationing and I t   ht 'good'!" The One woke up to how
angry she was by noticing h   action to the weather report. Then she
decided to find a new surg

What Brings Ones tc   erapy

It was easy to find One   o were familiar with the Enneagram
and who had experienced p   otherapy. Many have made personal
growth efforts through bo   r psycho-educational venues before
they reach a therapist's of   Their interest in self-improvement,
their trust in external aut   ty and their often painful internal
landscape all make them re   ve to changework. The exceptions to
this are Ones who project t   nternal critic onto the perceived evil
of others. Comfortable in th   go-saint" position, these individuals
don't seek therapy except t   prove the people around them.
Although not referring   e Enneagram, the following passage
from Marion Woodman's b   *Addiction to Perfection*, nicely captures
the underlying pain of the   ectionist character style: "Living by
principles is not living your   life. It is easier to try to be better than
you are than to *be* who you   f you are trying to live by ideals, you
are constantly plagued by a   e of unreality. Somewhere you think
there must be some joy: it ca   e all 'must,' 'ought to,' 'have to.' And
when the crunch comes, yo   re to recognize the truth: you weren't
there. Then the house of c   collapses. In trying to live out your
principles and ideals, the   that matters the most was lost. The
hideous irony then has t   faced." (1982, p. 61) This kind of
existential crisis, accompan   y symptoms of depression and loss,
sometimes brings Ones to   py.

What Does Not Work

Ones said that the two most common mistakes therapists made were either colluding with the One's righteous story line or too quickly challenging the One's inner critic. Because they are hyper-alert to criticism, Ones may perceive a therapist's interpretations as more negative than intended. In transference, Ones may either ideal-ize or criticize the therapist; idealization can inhibit the client's honesty, while being critical can lead them to abandon therapy.

Under stress, Ones are unaware of the intense anger that they radiate. They can look tense and rigid, perhaps frowning or with a tight jaw. Their rigidity and moral projection can cause others to feel on guard or criticized. Caught in counter-transference, a One's thera-pist could feel defensive, irritated or anxious.

Ones may not trust the therapeutic process until they have enough information and understand "the rules." This may provide a safe framework for tolerating therapy's risks. If a therapist ignores this need, therapy can come to a premature and unnecessary end: "I was in analytic therapy and the therapist kept asking me about my fantasies about her. I was afraid and would cut it off by saying I didn't see that had anything to do with it. I asked her to give me material, a textbook or something, to explain to me why that was important. She wouldn't. This was an impasse. I couldn't move forward and I quit.

"It was too bad, because I feel she could have reached the deep feelings I needed to experience. It was just too scary to take it further without more information."

Ones want therapists to understand how hard it is for them to ask for what they need. If they do and the request is denied, especially without explanation, the One may feel ashamed and withdraw.

Ones are also sensitive to ethical concerns and a therapist who overlooks this risks losing their trust: "I lost confidence in my thera-pist when he violated the confidentiality of someone else and then tried to make it seem justified. To feel safe, I needed to know the therapist was ethical, even though I knew he was talented."

Ones are authority compliant, usually polite and often seem strong, all of which can blind therapists to their vulnerability. Thera-pists who overlook this may find their One clients quit with minimal discussion: "My therapist could not see how vulnerable I was, she kept going in a direction she wanted to and was not picking up on my cues. I had to leave then." Ones recommend that therapists listen for polite answers – "no, that is not it" – and avoid getting attached to therapeutic strategies or ideas that may be misguided or premature.

Ones offered the foll[...]g tips for recognizing when they are defended in therapy:

- "I can be tightly rig[...]us and quite convincing about all the ways my position is corre[...]nd that may have nothing to do with what I need someone to u[...]stand."
- "I can be sarcastic o[...]ch more rarely, explosive with anger, attacking others and listin[...]ir wrongs."
- "I can be self-depre[...]g and apologetic."
- "When I'm defend[...]'m rigid and tight, emotionally and physically. I translate my [...] and insecurity into being angry with others. Then I turn my ang[...]ack on me because I do not like how I am behaving. I'm less abl[...]rticulate what I am feeling because I need to dig down to my r[...]elings. I may be ashamed of them, or think I shouldn't have the[...]
- Ones can also be cha[...]g and intellectual, quickly shifting the conversation to interestir[...]bjects to avoid feelings: "I may be intellectual and engaging[...]nversationally leading the therapist around to touch on differe[...]ics but avoiding staying with any real issue."
- "I saw a therapist w[...] was depressed and wanted to change my pattern of switching a[...]ions to cope. I really liked this thera-pist, but we did not work [...] anything real. I was intellectualizing, monkey-minding and got [...]y with it. Even though I put it on the table with her in the beginn[...]nd said: 'I'll be tough to help, it is hard for me to get to my feelin[...]he never nailed me. It was just like a friendly chat."

What Does Work

Ones had a lot to say [...]ut what worked for them in therapy. Many mentioned the value [...]arning to trust the process rather than achieving goals: "Before [...]py, I had done lots of self-improve-ment, where you set a goa[...]l figure out how to get there. The real work in therapy was abo[...]ing in the process, regardless of out-come, and learning it is n[...]out control." Other Ones said it was important that the therapy [...]a dependable schedule and structure: "At first my husband and [...]ere just going occasionally. It helped more to set a regular tim[...]ive me a structure on which I could depend."

For Ones who may l[...]difficulty knowing how they feel or what they should feel, a th[...]ist's ability to interpret and articulate feelings can help: "One thi[...]y therapist did was to pose a possibility about whatever I was feeling and ask if that fit. Sometimes it did and sometimes it didn't. When it did, it really helped me formulate what was going on inside me." Another One appreciated patience: "What helps me is patient, persistent guiding – helping me find my way to what I am afraid to face. Use logic and non-judgmental questions with an attitude of interest and caring."

Ones reported that cognitive and educational approaches helped them learn when they are feeling overly responsible as well as how to set boundaries. Since Ones focus on doing things right, taking appropriate action and finding balance are often subjects in therapy: "I am not afraid to take a stand, to risk articulating what I think is just and fair. It can be a lonely path, in part self-imposed. My concerns and values seem so different from those of many others. I don't mean that to sound arrogant, it's just the feeling of being apart, the stranger at the party. And part of my path has been to determine how and when and if I 'should' make an effort to engage, or if it is OK not to – *to do what I want.* Scary words. A constant and difficult part of my growth is learning to let go, to detach, to realize I cannot control things. Also to open my heart, to not be so guarded or closed to taking emotional risks."

Because a One's attention is usually focused on what they are *not* doing well, it helps when therapists recognize and applaud their progress: "There is this goal orientation, I want to see progress and be rewarded. I see it as all or nothing, and I want to be validated for what I have done. I would argue with positive feedback; but it mattered. The therapist made me listen so I could hear it and feel it. I had to stop my head and fill myself with the feelings of the heart and body. It's never enough in my head. In my heart and body it is enough."

When working with Ones, it's important to remember that they are gut-based people who act as if they are head-based people. Ones I interviewed often suggested that therapists help them identify the physical signs of emotions – the body sensations connected to emotional states. For example, some Ones said that when they were emotionally angry they physically felt, "invincible, like the Incredible Hulk," or as if they were wearing a "cloak of righteousness."

Similarly, other habitual inner states – being self-critical, for instance – have an associated physiology that can be identified and worked with. Asking One clients to tune in to their body feelings can shift their focus off their "shameful" anger and can help them adopt a more neutral attitude of self-observation. It can also help them link their current immediate reactions to habitual driving emotions and childhood beliefs.

To be successful, therap⟩ in some way, since, as one ɪ words for anger as Eskimos h with the anger hidden in rɛ might, for instance, have to be things about someone who h people in the same situation ᴠ cally put a positive spin on th spin is unconscious and feeː response. However, it can leɛ

Exploring with Ones hoᴠ fairness and goodness can heː feelings. But they have to trusɪ of perfection – judged by the tʰ

When you give feedbac formation, be aware of the Or exposes a One client's dispɔ may react with denial, defensi between what they feel and ᴠ need to understand how dev One good way to approach direct, saying something like: This tact and tone can enliɛ observe themselves.

The anger in a One's ɪ specific complaints or take tʰ tion is a feeling most Ones wi low-grade anger that feels juɛ Angry Ones can devalue the being unfair.

For better or for worse, (mind and it creates an enerɡ therapist had me close my eyɪ to let go of the story and juɛ returned my attention to the tant, at least for a while. Part c behavior than my own need tɪ my energy and examine the ɛ

Working directly with ar ship can free a One from sɛ transition from neurotically ɪ world as it is. They also connɛ

⟩nes will have to address anger ɪent said, "Ones have as many ɪnow." But, working effectively formation is challenging. You with a One client who says good ᴠounded them. Although most ɪact with anger, Ones automati- ɪtially unjustified feelings. This than risking a more authentic ɪrs feeling confused.

ɪ to have to uphold standards of admit their true and immediate ɪy won't be judged by standards ɪ the way they judge themselves. Ɔne who is caught in reaction ɪg internal critic. If the therapist ɪ anger prematurely, the client and shame – furthering the split ɪy "should" feel. Therapists also ɪ Ones think their own anger is. ɪ formation is to be gentle and ɪou to notice something here…" ɪne's ability to dispassionately

formation may bubble up in of generalized irritation. Irrita- ɪously admit to, as it is a kind of ɪd supports self-righteousness. ɪs of their scorn and rationalize

ɪ a lot done in an angry state of ʰerapists can work with: "My ɪst feel my body. He guided me ɪe power of my anger. When I ɪ my anger, it was not so impor- ɪus on another is less about their ɪs anger. It is good for me to own ɪt I attach to it."

ɪe safety of the therapy relation- ɪsed restrictions. It helps them ɪ control life to appreciating the ᴠing issues that are unrelated to their presenting problem.

A One's resentments often conceal their hidden desires. An angry One may, in fact, want to be appreciated, express sadness, or have more pleasure and fun. It is not unusual for Ones who are resentful of others to be stumped by the question, "What do *you* want?" Because having personal needs may expose them to judgment or humiliation, Ones can be frightened to admit them, even to themselves. Therapists may need to reassure Ones that it's normal to have needs and even satisfy them.

When Ones recognize and experience their own true but displaced feelings, their resentful storylines melt away. A couple I worked with, for example, was struggling with their blended family. The wife was a One and the husband a Three. The presenting issue, according to the One, was the "needy and immature behavior" of her husband's daughter. After the One resentfully detailed the child's "behavioral problems," I asked her if she wanted something that the child was getting. The woman began to cry and softly said, "Attention." The therapy then refocused on the One's difficulty with admitting her own needs and expressing them to her husband. Her anger and criticism had pushed him away. When the husband understood what his wife needed, he responded with warmth and attention. The subject of the child was dropped.

Shifting a One client from their head to their physical sensations, especially to feel their heart, can bring a flood of emotions, most notably grief. Many Ones recommended ways of getting out of their minds and into their feelings: bodywork, massage, breath work, dance and drumming. Some also mentioned painting, especially when it's done for self-expression rather than to master the skill.

All such practices can help a One become more receptive. When reported symptoms are troubling and don't improve with insight work or cognitive strategies, it can be beneficial to use approaches designed to work with the unconscious. These include: hypnosis techniques such as an affective bridge or spontaneous recall imagery, EMDR (see Chapter Two), and work with dissociation. When skillfully applied to symptoms that seem intractable, these methods can provide remarkable transitions.

Helping a One uncover childhood beliefs and repressed experiences may yield important information and promote change: "Uncovering the truth was helpful, as was learning about myself, making sense of the inexplicable and beginning to be able to understand and forgive myself. Without memory recovery work, I would not be where I am today. It gave me context, understanding, and the oppor-

tunity to continue to grow al
unbiased, wise, non-judgme
safe place to just be."
Other Ones recommend
taneity, taking vacations, fu
create a space in the One's l
from being encouraged to br
tionists to occasionally be "b
Enneagram-savvy Ones
system: "The therapist knew
supported. Even when she s
honest without being judgme
with myself." And learning
also helpful: "Learning abou
mental framework for suppc
nations and options for conti
framework, in the types, for u
and the people I love."

Working With the Inner (
While defusing a One's i
many ways to work with it in
successfully used gentle iror
talk about how it seems to be
your side?" Teaching a One
dialogues with it, perhaps t
promote insight. If the client
suggest that they allow thei
margins or write them with a
Ones may also need to
and their inner critic: "Ther
knowing, which comes with
petty and agitated." Encour
their critic has been in the
vigilance – can also lighten t
Bly poem, "One Source of B
the misinformed inner child
Asking a One's inner
perspective can also create a s
a way to detach from rur
Vipassana, a type of Buddhis
and feelings come and go, no

myself. It was like finding an
ding board and a completely

ierapists support "play, spon-
ne in nature." Such activities
enity. Some Ones also benefit
iles; it can be good for perfec-
rmless ways.
vhen their therapist knew the
ie. I felt accepted, cared for and
iave work to do too.' She was
this helped me be more gentle
ut their Enneagram style was
ieagram gave me a non-judg-
derstanding, as well as expla-
earn and grow. I also found a
iling relationships with myself

c can seem daunting, there are
A One client said her therapist
r, saying things like, "Can we
i for you if your therapist is on
iame the inner critic and have
ile-playing or journaling, can
ialing, a therapist may want to
itic to make comments in the
colored pen like a book editor.
ih between their self-observer
d me learn to trust my inner
iody. By contrast, my critic is
ies to appreciate how helpful
vhile questioning its present
I sometimes share the Robert
iation," which addresses how
iave your life."
ee an issue from the heart's
i also mentioned meditation as
esentful thoughts: "Through
in, I learned to let my thoughts
but not trying to contain them

or judge them. It helped me see through the critical illusion of reality I habitually construct and appreciate my life as it actually unfolds." Any other method that allows Ones to detach from the harsh driving aspect of their inner critic would also be helpful.

Mary Oliver's poem "Wild Geese" is especially relevant for Ones. The first line, "You do not have to be good," is followed by, "You do not have to walk on your knees for a hundred miles through the desert, repenting." Although these insights may be obvious to other Enneagram styles, they are good news for Ones.

Family of Origin and Relationship Work

Mapping a One client's family of origin can help them recognize repetitive patterns and understand their defenses. Ones may, however, have idealized their family and resist talking about them out of fear of being unfair or disloyal.

Reminding the One client that what they say in therapy is confidential can help them talk about difficult issues without betraying the good. It's also helpful to reassure them that the point of examining the impact of childhood situations is not to judge the intentions of others. A One reported how her therapist helped her feel safe enough to face her difficult early life: "She had me visualize a magical container, to store sweet qualities of my family members, and place it where it couldn't be damaged should any negativity surface during the therapy session."

Some Ones recommended group therapy: "We Ones feel invisible and need recognition. Groups can be helpful, but not if they're task-oriented." Like Threes, Ones need to focus on their feelings rather than their "doings." Groups also replicate relationship patterns and, if handled skillfully, can help Ones become aware of family dynamics and relationship patterns.

Ones are afraid that their world will fall apart if they aren't hyper-vigilant. The support one client received in family therapy enabled her to concentrate on her own work: "Having the therapist hold other family members accountable allowed me to just take care of myself. The therapist took charge of putting things into words; this was usually my job. She would ask my husband hard questions and this helped me see that I needed to take responsibility to look inside and I had the freedom to do so. I had avoided looking inward by taking care of everyone else. Inside, the first layer was fear and anxiety. I couldn't avoid it – I had to be there. None of the old stuff worked. This was the hardest time of my life, but I discovered a true inner power that I hadn't known was there. The blustery external power was

covering my fear. My fear w   )eing enough in every situation.
Seeing this was spiritual. I   ling to trust things that I don't
have words for. My need to   ings into concepts is an intellectual exercise. I moved fror   ig the rules of the structure to
trusting the process."

In couples therapy, O   attach new grievances to old
resentments. Not surprising   ignificant others can experience
this as stressful. When a Or   n hurt, a sincere apology by the
other person as well as a ch   eir behavior are usually crucial
or the relationship won't m   rd. When this is not enough, the
weary still-blamed partner   ess defensive if the therapist can
help unveil the vulnerabilit   ves the One's anger.
Bruce Fischer, who cre   )ivorce Adjustment Seminars,"
developed a "self-encounte   e," a journaling technique that I
sometimes recommend to (exercise starts with a concrete
description of the issue, rati   uch emotional charge it has and
how important it is on a sc   he writer is asked to note their
associated body sensation   ughts. Their "inner child" and
"inner-critic" are each invit   e their perspective of the issue,
which often links to old wo   "wise nurturing" aspect of the
person is also invited to cor   id this is followed by creating a
plan of action. I find this ex   n helps the client acknowledge
the deeper layers of the wo   iccess the higher perspective of
the observing ego. This s   leads the One to admit their
vulnerable emotions and a   iacy.
While Ones can be slo   ve, they are usually anxious to
end any discussion about t   uences of their own damaging
behavior. In relationships,   to resist negative feedback by
rationalizing or aggressivel   ing in a way that prevents them
from hearing about their mi   eir old childhood pain at feeling
criticized is well-armored. '   pist helped me learn to tolerate
feedback and listen empath   a One reported. "It also helped
when my husband reassur   t he still saw the good in me."
Therapists doing relati   ork with Ones might remember
that they resist letting in n   ation once they have formed a
rigid position. In some cases   ng a separate individual session
so a One can ventilate fe   side the conjoint therapy can
prevent damage to the re   . It is important to keep this
balanced, however, to avc   ing the One is the "identified
patient." Ones want to be   uraging them to listen to their
bodies, to take time to refl   than react, will lead them to a

deeper honesty.

To help Ones get past their rigid, one-right-way thinking, encouraging them to "brainstorm" may be effective. When solving a problem ask them to write down all possible scenarios and options. No idea is too wild or bad to be included. This technique opens a pathway to a One's vision and creativity.

As Ones outgrow their righteous false self and its damaging behavior, they develop genuine humility and compassion. At this point, therapeutic strategies that help Ones detach from their perfect persona and appreciate the perspective of others are useful. Psychodrama techniques or role-playing that uses role reversal often facilitate this shift. A therapist might ask a One client to close her eyes and remember a difficult interpersonal encounter. Next the therapist asks the One to imagine being the other person, and to notice any difference in her experience or reactions. This kind of exercise can help the client become more empathic and evaluate whether she is communicating the messages she intends to communicate.

In his book *Transformation Through Insight*, Claudio Naranjo narrates part of a Gestalt therapy session with a One. Describing the outcome, he comments, "I also think the session remarkable for how much insight she gained into the cruelty involved in her goody-goody perfectionistic self." Another One client recalls a similar insight: "An experience in 'accidental art therapy' brought my perfectionism home to me. I was doing a charcoal self-portrait from a mirror while ruminating about some individuals whom I resented. It was a shock to see the righteousness in the portrait and to understand that it was the person whom the subjects of my resentment saw, rather than the idealized self I imagined."

Compassion and Forgiveness

When working with painful memories and relationships that bring up the need to forgive, Ones cautioned therapists to "remind us that forgiveness does not mean making something okay. It's enough to explore what forgiveness may mean. Self-forgiveness is most difficult and transformative."

Getting Ones past self-chastising and helping them become more compassionate towards themselves can be the cornerstone of treatment. My husband/partner John Reynolds, who works often with people with war trauma, described a One client who was a medic in Vietnam: "This man struggled with pervasive shame and guilt that seemed intractable. In one session I suggested that the client visualize himself at age nineteen, the age he was in Vietnam, on one side of the

room and then se
room. Eyes closed
the shame since tl
move towards an
gained through th
tive that helped
himself." Childhc
forgive themselve

It can be dif
everything right t
and other losses c
with self-sacrifice.
ness in the face o
them to see a la
depressed after s
position of havin;
side. But it just dic
valid than anyone
my grief. This bro
understand that t
concrete facts."

Another On
divorce, said: "I l
Understanding hi
was true and vali
could only be in
excruciating, but
doing the best th
accept their own l

Connecting P
One Connects t

The One's cor
to a One's restric
must be earned ai

The emotion
One's creativity ai
territory may seer
cality. They somet
in this ego state. M
a difficult and in

nternalized shame on the other side of the
ient could see that he had been on the side of
. We then worked on what it would take to
race his nineteen-year-old self. The insight
rvention seemed to bring a shift in perspec-
ent accept his circumstances and forgive
tures and memorabilia can also help Ones
soften their judgments.

or Ones who have spent a lifetime doing
things go wrong. Divorce, illness, betrayals
el like a confusing violation of their contract
apist may need to sit with the One's helpless-
mingly unfair and unjust world and guide
cture and accept multiple truths. A One,
t a lawsuit, said: "I was so caught in my
everything right and the facts were on my
tter in the end. It didn't make my truth more
Therapy helped me find compassion through
e to a new depth of understanding. I could
tional truths of others were as valid as my

njoint therapy, with a husband considering
sit with the tension of the contradictions.
and feeling my anger, and knowing all of it
here was nothing I could do. I had to learn I
ocess and not control the outcome. It was
ned my heart." Realizing that everyone is
and no one is perfect can allow the One to
ity.

:

ns to both Four and Seven provide antidotes
s, undercutting their belief that any desire
erved.
ities of their connection to Four enhance a
yment of spiritual belonging. However, this
ngruent with the One's goal-directed practi-
ncounter dispossessed aspects of themselves
scribe it as valuable if uncomfortable: "It was
nt place for me to open to. My therapist

supported me to stay there. This helped me see the potential for learning and growing by allowing feelings that seemed self-indulgent, like sadness and specialness. She helped me work with my shame and see there is merit in this vulnerability and it enhanced my capacity to be with another person. This is the only place I got it."

Getting in touch with their true feelings may have ramifications in a One's relationships: "With some of my friends I had been a caretaker and had only expressed my cheerful Seven connection. When I allowed more of my darker emotions to come through, some of my old friends didn't want to be around me. Therapists need to coach us on how to be vulnerable in the world and survive." The longing to love and the fear of abandonment stirred up by the connection to Four can open a One's heart, both emotionally and spiritually.

On the down side, Ones can get stuck in feeling "bad and flawed" possibly in a melodramatic way. Behind all their good intentions, Ones can be overly sensitive, personalize slights and withdraw into Four-like depression.

One Connects to Seven

The One's connection to Seven brings a capacity for expansive, positively directed fantasy: "During therapy I learned I could fantasize and let go of being more practical, or correct, or P.C. This was a gift that has stayed with me." Ones report a lighter, freer and more fun perspective on life is available to them when they connect to Seven. They say they experience this aspect of self much of the time when they are on vacation.

On the down side, Ones, like Sevens, can be driven by their fear of staying with emotional difficulty. They can also become rigid about positive thinking, policing themselves and others for negative attitudes. Or, the ego states of One and Seven can function together to justify a sense of license. This can help Ones rationalize self-indulgence even when their behavior hurts others.

Dreams

Dreams can help bring Ones into a more honest experience of their feelings, although a therapist may have to remind them that their dreams have many levels of meaning – archetypal, as well as personal. As Jeremy Taylor, a well-known dream worker, says: "All dreams come in the service of health and wholeness, including nightmares." A compassionate therapist whom the One trusts is essential for this work because the dream images that represent

repressed ne
A One v
anxiously rej
ocean carryii
apparently n
were spilling
was afraid tł
After th
about anger v
to overcome

Good Enc

Ones cai
safety of ther
and grieved;
feelings – ca
compassion f
can be observ
with their wł
Christian no
earn it."
In a con\
to awaken cc
day when I i
together and
flaws. That w
being presen
help.

feelings can be stark and overwhelming.
s trying to contain her anger towards her family
the following dream: "I was walking along the
iefcase. Bloody body limbs of some people I had
ed were in it. The briefcase fell open, the limbs
nd I was burying them in the sandy beach. But I
n waves would surface them."
t shared this dream, she became more honest
r family. Therapeutic dream work can help Ones
and accept their needs and feelings.

Therapy

kenly believe that they are either bad or good. The
n allow their childhood wounds to be understood
ied parts of the self – including their needy angry
accepted. Compassion for themselves leads to
ers, and softens a One's judgment. Relationships
n a wider screen. As Ones grow more comfortable
lf, their "comparing minds" are less vigilant. The
grace is especially relevant: "You don't have to

on with Buddhist teacher Pema Chödrön on how
ion, the poet Alice Walker said, "I remember one
got it – that we are not as human beings joined
cted because of our perfections. It's because of our
h a relief." To relax into the serenity and joy of just
gift of this realization. Good enough therapy can

Twos

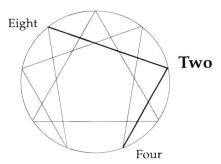

Eight

Two

Four

Presentat   in Therapy

- Two   ts can be engaging, seductive and flattering towards
therapists
- They   / be attractively dressed and use eye contact to
establish a v   , engaging relationship
- May   motional, prideful and sometimes histrionic
- Can   sconnected from their own needs
- Usuɛ   )cused on relationships and caretaking
- May   ɛ to therapy wanting to help significant others, or
bring them i   have the therapist work on them
- They   give without boundaries which often leads to a
panicky nee   ɨs, anger, exhaustion, and demands
- Subs   ɨ abuse: Despite their apparent social facility, many
Twos feel sc   ınxiety and report using substances before, during
and after soc   rents. The purpose is to repress unwelcome feelings.
As one Twc   ɨ: "My use of substances was always to mask my
feelings and   be nice. The drugs were a substitute for feelings."

Healthy   )s are in touch with their own feelings and easily
connect witɥ   ɨrs in an emotional way. They value themselves and
faithfully fol   vhat is in their own heart even as they recognize and
support the   in others.
When ɑ   ɪt in their unhealthy pattern, Twos "give to get,"

giving other people what they themselves want while hiding their expectation that others will reciprocate. Twos can become controlling, angry and resentful towards those they have over-accommodated. They lose touch with their own real feelings and needs, sometimes becoming indirect, disingenuous and manipulative. The Two attention style fixes on relationships, engagement with others, flattery, pleasing and supporting others selectively, being liked and looking good.

In many cultures the Two persona represents the archetypal female ideal. Being supportive, self-sacrificing and attentive to others are highly valued feminine traits. Male Twos are viewed with more ambivalence and may find that developing their connection to Eight (see Connecting Points) is a natural antidote to a feminized image.

Childhood Experiences and Adult Defenses

Two children have the inherent gift of emotional sensitivity and the ability to divine the needs of others. Sensitive and charming, the Two's ability to read others and engage them is evident from an early age. Knowing what others need and being uniquely equipped to provide it becomes a source of pride. As one Two said, "As a child, I knew things had to look good so I made my family look good."

A Two's Genogram will often indicate these qualities were unconsciously exploited by needy family members. A depressed yet gifted parent is a common practice ground for a future of over-attending to others: "My father was mildly depressed. It worsened and he became more withdrawn when I was an adolescent. I could see what he needed, and thought I could be a better wife to him than my mother." The Two child suppresses any feelings that might conflict with this giving role. The locus of control is on the person whom the Two wants to please.

In her book *Addiction to Perfection*, Marion Woodman describes the persona of someone fixated on pleasing others for survival: "If an individual is being fed and nourished emotionally by the mother – or a mother surrogate such as husband, company, Church, collective values – she is probably starving in relation to herself. She is dependent on the mother and therefore open to manipulation by the mother, vulnerable to her praise or rejection. She is not nourishing herself and her own feelings are being unrecognized or denied. She is starving. She has to perform perfectly in order to be loved. Her emotional stability is determined by another's reaction. On the one hand she is manipulated, on the other she is a manipulator because she has to be in order to be loved. She cannot depend on a love which accepts her for who she is. Whether the original manipulators are still in her life doesn't matter; they are alive in her psyche as complexes and if she isn't projecting them on her "loved ones," she is turning them against herself." (1982, p. 62) (1982, Woodman, M. *Addiction to Perfection: The still unravished bride.* Inner City Books.)

As Twos play helpful roles towards others they grow prideful, believing they have no needs of their own while knowing what's best for others. They maintain this pride through the defense mechanism of repression: the involuntary, automatic banishing of unacceptable ideas or feelings into the unconscious. Twos describe pride as an inflated emotional state in which the needs of others can be easily understood and met. Since pride is hard to identify from the inside, it is most likely not recognized until the Two experiences humiliation, its opposite feeling. For example, when others take from the Two but don't acknowledge the Two's contribution, or when others don't want what the Two is giving. It feels humiliating to be rejected or be caught having needs. At these times, the Two's aggressive – or even vengeful – side might surface, often to the surprise of others.

When Twos repress their feelings they deny being a vulnerable person with normal needs. One Two saw this keenly when her marriage broke up: "At the end of my first marriage on the day we decided to divorce, I was telling my soon to be ex-husband I was angry because I always did what he wanted. He worked, I stayed home, I made our home beautiful, cooked a lot, and arranged our social life, all because he wanted me to. He acted like he wasn't interested. I didn't really want to do these things and I had put my desires aside. He looked at me and said 'I never wanted you to do those things – I never asked you to do those things.' I got really defensive at first; I didn't want him to tell me that those things didn't mean anything.

"Weeks later I realized he never had asked me for those things although I could have sworn he had. I wanted to be like everyone else and I had married the most steady and dependable person I could, completely repressing who I was. I had become who and what I thought he wanted me to be. All along I thought he appreciated what I was doing for him."

Another Two commented: "I repressed how competitive and mean-spirited my younger sister was. I needed to believe there was someone else for me. I was big enough to be the angel for both of us. I made her into the sister I needed and loved that effigy. I had to keep repressing lots of things to support my illusion. Idealizing the relationship served my pride I had saved her. I now understand she perceived my role quite differently. When I saw through my illusion to how it really was I found that I don't even like her all that much. But we are able to have a more honest relationship now."

What Brings Twos to Therapy

Some Twos come to therapy depressed, exhausted and frustrated that all their efforts in relationships have not led to getting their own needs met. Therapy offers Twos the possibility of having their own needs recognized and they are often genuinely motivated to understand their compulsion to repress their own needs.

Several Twos said they were introduced to therapy through family counseling where another family member was the identified patient. It is hopeful and exciting for Twos to work through their conflicts in the context of relationships, since this is familiar territory for them. One Two recalled: "My first therapy experience was when my whole extended family participated in my sister's in-patient treatment. I thought, this is the place for me; I knew I wanted to do this kind of work – I'd be good at it." Another adds: "My first therapy experience was in family counseling. Our oldest son was having substance abuse problems and when he went in-patient I went on a learning curve about family dynamics."

Some Twos identify with descriptions of "The Imposter Syndrome" and admit that while their focus on relationships has helped them succeed, it does not always feel genuine. If a Two's family included a critical or competitive parent, their present successes can feel like failures: "I was getting so much recognition in my work, people love me and I can work a room, yet I keep hearing my dad say 'you are such a liar.' The anxiety and shame is right behind the recognition." Another Two added: "I had a great marriage and two beautiful daughters; I won a prestigious writing award, yet something felt strange inside. I had never talked to anyone about my mom's alcoholism and I didn't know what normal was. I heard my mom's voice saying 'you snowed them.' I was depressed and began therapy to deal with it."

What Does Not Work

Twos are often natural healers and many find their way into the helping professions. They identify with the care-giving role and may be critical of a therapist's skill: "I was watching the therapist thinking, I should be sitting there. I revered her knowledge and position but after a while I realized she wasn't getting to feelings."

Another Two recalled: "I read a lot of books and I knew I over-functioned. My husband and I saw a marriage counselor six times. In this time I realized I set the counselor up to be on my side against my husband. I could see him look at me for approval. I got it, this is what always happened in our relationship. I confronted the therapist on the last session and laid it out. We weren't going back, I saw what was going on, and I was going to change on my own."

The warmth and interpersonal skills of the Two client can present a challenge in the treatment relationship. The client may flatter the therapist or counselor into thinking they are wonderful. If a therapist starts to feel special during a session, it is a good idea to become particularly alert to transference and counter-transference. We all have vulnerabilities and Twos are particularly talented at sensing someone's wound and acting as its healer. It is difficult for the helper to be helped.

The Two's focus on relationships may also lead to boundary confusion. Many Two clients I spoke to reported a pattern of ineffective client-therapist relationships where professional boundaries grew unusually fuzzy. This was noticeably more common than for other Enneagram styles.

This tendency reminded me of a charismatic Two I treated early in my practice. Raised in a difficult family, she had been in therapy since she was a young woman. In the first session she talked about her history of treatment with several psychotherapists and counselors. Each had become her personal friend or professional collaborator, either during or following treatment. As I listened I thought, with some regret, how she would be a wonderful friend, warm and perceptive. Then I explained the professional boundaries and their purpose. She did deep and long-term work and later mentioned that it had been a relief in the beginning to know she would not have to become my friend!

The weak boundaries of a talented yet wounded therapist caused another Two considerable confusion: "I wanted to work with a famous group therapist. I called him and tried to sell myself. I remember trying to be appealing enough, easy but interesting, for him to want to work with me. He recognized the needs and wants issue right away. He was able to fulfill them some, but also help me work with the tension and see the old family dynamics. I appreciate the risks he took. Unfortunately, he became inappropriately involved with someone I had become friends with through the group. She told me in secret and asked me not to tell even when I said it would be important for my therapy to be able to talk about it. It seemed around that time that he distanced from me, which felt like part of the triangle. It took a year to leave the group and it was painful. I'm still sorting it out. I still long for the resolution that putting it on the table might have brought. The triangle and secrets were awful but much of the work was helpful."

To effectively diminish counter-transference, therapists of Twos need to closely attend to the feelings they experience in the relationship and observe any unspoken content. If a therapist does not keep good boundaries, therapy can become a powerful, unfortunate replay of a family drama in which the therapist is seduced into a dual relationship.

Twos usually do not suffer from a lack of friends and lovers. However, offering them a friendly and accepting relationship is important. "I have to know the therapist likes me," one Two said, echoing many others: "I need a lot of positive affirmation without having to ask for it." "To be liked feels like basic safety."

Other stories included therapists who did not understand the Two's worldview or were impatient and counterproductively directive:

• "I went to therapists who told me not to believe or feel what I do. The attitude was 'just get over it.' This comes across as a demand or an expectation, and sets me up to comply one more time, to caretake or adapt to the therapist."

• "Some therapists have a hard time waiting for their Two clients to realize they have needs and wants. They might see it as a martyr thing and not realize how hard the Two is trying."

• "I am the peacemaker, in an over-functioning role with my family and my husband's family. My mother-in-law would call and say 'good, I got ya' and I was trapped. My therapist needed to hear me and see how I was over functioning. She never got it. I needed help with boundaries."

• "The therapist was cold, just took notes and made no eye contact."

• "One therapist said, 'it's not like you are going to die if you don't have love.' I felt again my inherent need to love and be loved was worthless. I felt rejected. She didn't understand me and I never went back."

Some Twos can idealize their therapists or see them as omniscient: "I was frustrated. I admired my therapist and knew he knew my mind better than I did. I had to try to get into his mind to learn what he knew about me.

"I always feared I would be bothering him if I wanted to have an extra session or call between sessions. I thought I should be able to make it a week or these meetings would be closer than a week. It would have been good if he could have told me that there might be times when once a week won't be enough and for those times you can call. He would have had to say it when I wasn't hurting though, like it was normal information to consider when I need it if I do."

Several Two clients told of therapists who failed to understand their depth of pain. The Two's charm and implicit pride, especially about relationships, can effectively mask their needs. Since they may look better than they feel and match perceived expectations, a therapist can misjudge them. It may help to know what Twos say about how they appear when they are defended in therapy:

• "I present with ironic humor. Sometimes grief and despair make me sound sharper-edged."

• "I would let you know some ways I've been successful."

• "I would take everything personally."

• "I always look pulled together and put up a good front."

• "What therapists have missed when they try to work with me is that I can look good and function well and that doesn't reflect the depth of my pain."

• "I can talk most therapists blue. I have a need to be liked and I want to tell them what is going to make them like me. I want to belong. It's very split, on one side incredibly disappointing because I really want to move. On the other hand it is comforting. I get reinforcement and support. They would never know I was disappointed."

• "I'm not particularly good with boundaries and what I'm responsible for. I'm trying to please and I'm sensitive to the therapist being pleased or not."

Other Twos were aware of taking care of their therapists:

• "I went to a therapist for some time. It wasn't helping and I knew it but I kept going because I didn't want to hurt his feelings."

• "Even when in my gut I feel a therapist is not good, then even when they show I'm right, I hang in and try to help them."

• "I had protected my old family therapist, softened the truth about his inappropriate behavior. I called him to confront him and he didn't hear me. I feel like I could do the guy some good, so why doesn't he want this from me?"

These stories might surprise a therapist who is being idealized – or manipulated – by a Two client. As mentioned, Twos will flatter and try to please the therapist in an effort to be special and therefore safe. This underscores the difficulty and importance of getting honest feedback from these clients.

What Does Work

Several Twos said they wanted therapists to ask them how they feel rather than assuming they are fine because they look fine. They recommended that therapists assign writing between sessions, perhaps by saying something like: "Sometimes it takes a while for people who are very tuned into the needs of others to realize what they themselves feel. In the next week I want you to write about anything that might help me work with you. Please include anything that we are not discussing that we should be talking about. This may be difficult, but doing so will help." Therapists can also use a Two's helpful impulses to double-bind them, for example by saying: "Telling me the truth about how this is going is a way you can help me to do good work."

In therapy, the relationship is always a large part of what helps clients heal. This is especially pertinent with Twos; their wound is about relationship and so is the medicine: "Going to therapy is good practice for asking for help. You can have every feeling in the world and be accepted. My therapist says 'you cry every tear' and it is all good, nourishing and healing." Another Two said: "I saw a guy from the University. I don't know exactly what he did, but one day after a session I was driving and realized I was so angry I could cause a nuclear explosion. I pulled over and just sobbed. I then realized it would take everything I had to just damage one small room! He just invited me to know myself, asked me questions I had never been asked and then listened." Another client reported: "My Hakomi therapist is also Buddhist. He is gentle and direct. His attentiveness is exquisite. My self-concept has grown. I feel he sees me and responds to who he sees with compassion and respect. He has a sense of humor about the world and has helped me to distance."

Offering well-timed basic information can also help: "My best counselor was soft and sweet and direct. I always felt safe with her. It was hard to admit I'd hurt my daughter and it was ten times harder to admit she had hurt me. I had to look at how I denied my anger. My therapist said 'resentment is anger turned inward.' She helped me turn it around and look at the truth."

The client's belief that therapy will help also predisposes a positive outcome: "I set my last therapist up to succeed. I said 'I know this is going to work.'" A therapist's humility can support progress as well: "It was really important to me that he established a relationship with me before we did anything scary. I did a long take-home questionnaire and the therapist never brought it up. Finally I brought it up with him. He had forgotten. It was like catching the teacher making a mistake and it allows me to be more human. There was a lot of laughter in the relationship. It was helpful to know there wasn't a right way to do it. He validated that what had been done to me was wrong. One time I went in and just cried for the whole session. It was OK with him and that was important."

Working with Pride

Good therapy with Twos will inevitably confront their pride. Pride creates a competitive, sometimes subtle dynamic in a Two's relationships. Others can feel overwhelmed by the way the Two casts them into subordinate roles while saving the special job of special care deliverer for themselves. Ironically, this can bring others to distance themselves from the Two to keep from being overwhelmed and "managed." Twos say that learning to recognize the negative impact of pride on their relationships is an important but difficult step. Then they can begin to understand their own motivation: "I'm getting a grip on when I'm protecting and inflating others and learning to ask myself 'who is this really good for?'"

After a Two's pride is recognized, the needs it covers may also be exposed. The therapist can then help the client accept their human vulnerability. Several Twos talked about how this feels and what they wanted from their therapists:

• "Therapists need to understand how shame plays an enormous role in having needs and wants. The shame is for not meeting the wants and needs of others perfectly."

• "I need to forgive myself for having needs."

• "We Twos don't like to admit we have icky feelings. Help us know that they are normal."

• "As a Two, I really need to respect the therapist. The therapist needs to very gently confront my behavior, they could say something to me like: 'It seems like you really want to impress me, how would it be if I wasn't impressed with you?'"

Another Two explained how her therapist gently helped her see through her pride to recognize her underlying fears: "When I'm intuiting and meeting the needs of others, I'm really empty and desperate. I would say how nice her office was, how nice her nails were, and she would just look at me intently. I always looked pulled together, and put up a good front. I was afraid of people knowing how black my soul was, so, I was a monk – so good, no anger. I had a secret life to handle my darkness, drugs and sex etc. My pride almost killed me. I saw the world was in such disarray and God has better things to do than worry about my life. It wasn't that bad for me, and I had no right to ask. My therapist challenged me to see my spiritual pride. She really encouraged a level of honesty in me. She was direct, and would say something like "in the Alcoholic family…" and I would know it was true for me too. She confronted my pride by telling me I wasn't powerful enough to make my mom drink. She helped me get to the place where I could still love myself when I was angry."

Twos admit that it is difficult for others to cut through their pride without provoking resistance. One man recommended that the therapist first "align with me, let me know how you see that I am right. Then present a different view, like 'Yeah, this is really great, and have you also thought of this other perspective?'"

It also helps Twos to learn to distinguish between the experience of pride and the experience of humility: "At first it was hard to understand the problem with pride. I wondered if it was wrong to be proud of my accomplishments, how well I have parented and how well my children are doing. I learned it is when I'm fooling myself that I'm doing something for another when it is really what I need. It is puffy in my chest. Pride has fear underneath it, it is an effort to find a place to stand, and it is competitive. Part of Two pride is not realizing how judgmental we are. Fear is the house of cards under the pride. I was giving out what I wanted from God.

"To know humility I had to get to a place where I could feel deeply beloved by God. Humility is being quiet. It is to be teachable, a quiet lake. Learning to ask myself 'what is the next right thing to do?' Trusting God, holy will."

Individual Talk Therapy

Exploring a Two's relationship history in talk therapy can yield rich clues about what keeps them from "getting the love they want." When they report conflicts with others through a filter of pride, Twos may sound martyr-like to the therapist, as though they are surrounded by unreasonable others who demand too much. Since some Twos are drawn to relationships with especially demanding people, it might be valuable to check whether they are accommodating the unrealistic expectations of others.

However, a Two's success at managing appearances can also lead therapists to discount or overlook the Two's more active role in creating relationship disappointments. For example, a people-pleasing Two might overbook her schedule and then stand people up. When others express displeasure, the Two may reframe this as insensitivity – failing to understand how important the Two's many commitments are. When Twos are caught in this pattern, relationships with people they already know may seem less enticing than new conquests.

While the point of a Two's giving is to be loved, the best candidates for authentic intimacy may distance themselves from a Two they can't count on. As a therapist elicits more detailed information, he or she may understand why others feel let down. The Two client could then be coached to examine their own behavior and, perhaps, learn to set limits. Sometimes clients who feel they must always please others need to learn to say "no." Then they can learn to say "yes" and really mean it.

The same dynamic could also arise in therapy. A Two could miss appointments or arrive late, deep in a crisis, offering compelling reasons for being delayed. The therapist is now having the same experience that others in the Two's life complain about. At such times, working directly with transference and counter-transference can be valuable. The therapist can offer honest feedback about how the Two's behavior feels and prompt the client to examine their underlying motivation.

Therapists can also explore with Twos why they are pursuing and giving to others from a distance. Why this relationship? This person? What feels juicy? Which relationships does the Two avoid? Which relationship stirs up resentment about having given too much? As one Two said: "It is very hard for me to look at my motives, I don't want to, but it is important."

If a Two client can experience a positive outcome from taking risks in therapy, this can be generalized to other relationships: "Treatment helped me 'get it.' That I have my own needs and wants, and can express them in my relationships."

Relationship Work

One inherent limitation of individual therapy is that it relies on self-reporting, so it is inevitable that the therapist gets a biased view. This is a point favored by therapists who prefer conjoint milieus. In conjoint or group settings, a Two's self-idealization can be confronted in a way that exposes its credibility gaps. When prideful Twos think they know what other people need, they proceed with their own agendas, blithely ignoring what the others actually say they want. As one Two explains: "I have an internal belief that if I apply myself to any relationship I can bring it around to where I want it." With the help of the therapist, group or family members can penetrate a Two's denial and help them see their behavior from an outside perspective. While it can be humiliating to confront their own insensitivity, in a group setting a Two can more easily admit their unconscious agendas and see their misguided efforts to make relationships a container for all needs. Also, when Twos quit pursuing and managing other people, they make space for the others to be who they are – rather than who the Two wants them to be. This makes authentic mutual relationships possible.

Some Twos mentioned that group work was especially helpful: "Watching others in a group being worked with, helped me know and empower myself." One obvious pitfall for Twos to avoid in group therapy is getting lost in the needs and stories of others. Their relational talents can keep them from getting their own needs met.

Working with Repression

As the safety of the therapeutic relationship increases, it is natural for Two clients to become more truthful: "I always got a little nurturing, but it took a long time to share that ugly withholding side." It is also likely that Twos will discover feelings of remorse and sadness about the price they have paid for all their helpful behavior. They may have to grieve the self they have lost, on the way to reclaiming it.

Twos want therapists to know how hard it is for them to recognize their own needs: "I want therapists to understand I am shame driven. I'm not willing or able to accept my own needs and wants, and I adapt to the needs and wants of others. I want a therapist to go for body feelings and process and to be patient with the resistance with the shift to myself." Another Two adds: "It is so forbidden to focus on myself and it feels like life and death to the kid inside." Twos also say that the therapy relationship itself can be corrective: "The relationship allowed me to know what I felt. Focusing on caring for others was automatic, but I had been through all this trauma and loss. I needed to focus on myself for a while."

Another Two described a physical role-playing exercise that provoked important insights: "My therapist had me push against her hands while she represented different people, my ex-husband, mother, father, boss. Each time she asked me 'how much resistance can you give?' I could see when I didn't push back, when I give my power away."

Many, though not all, Twos said that they ultimately needed more than talk therapy to get past their repression. "Talk therapy just did not get past my fixation. One time my therapist said we aren't going to talk anymore. You are just going to come here and do art. That is when I started to change." Some Twos mentioned being helped by alternative approaches: "Hakomi was the body-based approach I needed, it allowed me to accept the repressed parts of myself." Another added: "Transformational breath work allowed my repressed grief to surface."

Several Twos I interviewed mentioned the popular technique of "EMDR" or "Eye Movement Desensitization and Reprocessing." This technique, discovered and packaged by Francine Shapiro, is believed to re-pattern brain neuron pathways and alleviate trauma symptoms or phobias. Its best known intervention asks a client to remember a traumatic incident or phobic reaction and hold in place any associated sensations and thoughts. Then the client practices rapid open eye movements – following the therapist's moving fingers or a flashing light device – sometimes accompanied by sound or touch. For some, their experience of the trauma or phobia is dramatically transformed and neutralized.

Here are two stories with opposite outcomes from Twos who experienced EMDR. In the first, EMDR helped circumvent the relationship pitfalls: "This is the best therapy for me because I can't manipulate. I was over-involved with my daughters. One daughter was overweight and unhappy. I did EMDR. I pictured my daughter in a short shirt and big tummy, on one side. On the other, I pictured her boyfriend. When I moved my eyes I saw my family of origin and their disapproval when I was getting married and moving away. Eyes left I saw my parents, eyes right I saw my husband's parents. I realized my reaction to my daughter was really about my own left-over emancipation issues. I was able to let it go."

Another Two reported a less positive experience. The therapist used EMDR on the client's symptoms, but overlooked major issues: "I was in my fourth car accident, and I was in enormous pain, depression and insomnia and I was drinking alcoholically. I found someone who did EMDR, a wonderful therapist. But, what she worked with stayed compartmentalized. Each session I hoped she wouldn't ask about other areas of my life. She didn't and I always felt bad about that. I never revealed my drinking, or abusive marriage, though I would have."

One Two described how breaking through years of repression about childhood incest decreased her anxiety and compulsive connecting: "I'd been to several types of therapy over many years. There were always hints of incest in my childhood but I could never get clarity. There was this constant anxiety. Eventually I did some therapy using spontaneous recall imagery and remembered what had happened. It made so much sense, even though I didn't want to believe it, and I have been able to forgive myself so much. My anxiety is lessened. I'm able to let go of immediately attending to others just to avoid myself."

Consciously spending time alone is essential for Twos, both to face their fears of being disconnected from others and to reconnect with themselves. Learning to become comfortable with their own company also has spiritual and psychological benefits: "My therapist instructed me to take time for myself away from others and meditate. I would sit silently and just notice what surfaced on the screen in my mind. It was always relationship issues. After I did this for a while, the therapist had me practice letting them go."

Connecting Points
Two Connects to Four
Twos have a connection to Four and to Eight. In different ways these links encourage Twos to identify their needs and strengthen their boundaries.

The high side of the connection to Four is evident when Twos identify and interrupt their compulsive connecting and become more self-contained. This can initially be difficult because it brings up feelings of depression and abandonment. This is, however, when the deeper work of therapy can lead to a spiritual opening; as Twos get in touch with their needs they access the soulful part of themselves. To access the best of their Four connection, Twos suggested working with dreams, creative self-expression, journaling, poetry, and noticing what feelings surface when they are alone.

Here a Two explains her experience of both the high and low side of Four: "In Four, I'm more introverted. Gardening takes me there. I really just found this in the last decade. When I was young it was associated with depression and I resisted this part of myself, but I've discovered it is a pathway to knowing what I want. When I have alone time I remember how important it is. I've learned I crave it, though I never used to give it to myself. At first there was no feedback, no one telling me how nice I was. As I have more alone time I become more self-reliant."

Two Connects to Eight
Twos are often uncomfortable with their connection to Eight

because the aggression it brings is out of sync with their people-pleasing persona. When Twos repress their needs, their resentment can build up into a sense of entitlement, provoking Eight-like eruptions of impulsive anger. If they remember such outbursts later, Twos often feel embarrassed or ashamed by their behavior.

Developing a conscious connection to Eight is good medicine as it helps Twos accept what they want and know their boundaries. As one Two said: "Learning that having boundaries is not the same as being a bitch is important." Becoming appropriately assertive is a gift of the Two's connection to Eight: "Deep down I have a real need for honesty, directness and truth." Therapists can help Two clients identify the source of their anger as well as brainstorm new and more constructive choices for expressing it.

Twos are often comfortable in the role of protecting and advocating for others – a compassionate justice-seeking impulse also associated with the high side of Eight.

Dreams

Not surprisingly a Two's dream life often involves relationships. The following dream was reported by a Two who continued to say "yes" to other people's requests, despite the fact that she wanted more time for herself. She was growing increasingly resentful and felt trapped. This dream helped her see her despair and listen to her repressed needs: "I am with someone in the mountains and we are going somewhere on a train. We are in a huge boxcar full of people. Our car is stopped while others are allowed to continue. I keep running into people I don't want to see, we are all stuck together. I try to hide in a phone booth. A tall gray haired woman darts in also trying to hide. They are giving us no reason for holding us here. They won't let the train continue. I talk briefly to a man and am seductive with him, which makes me uncomfortable. I am caring for a baby. I look for my friend and think she must have talked her way out because she has an important job. Some have been allowed to leave and others not. I am told they have to promise not to tell who is left. I hope my friend will tell those who love me where I am. I yell at the people in control and demand to know why."

Good Enough Therapy

Good Enough Therapy offers the Two client a safe, nurturing relationship with clear boundaries. With the therapist's help, Two clients can examine their patterns and motivations as well as accept their underlying needs. This helps them individuate, to become their true self, independent of what others think. Letting go of the compulsion to be especially helpful – and therefore lovable – gives Twos the choice to nurture themselves as well as others. When their relationships are unmanaged they become more fulfilling and the Two gift of humility allows Twos to receive the genuine love and appreciation of others.

Threes

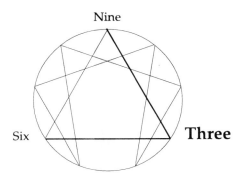

Presentation in Therapy

• Three clients can be busy workaholics; may readily list all the things they are doing; may speak in slogans or positive thinking cliches

• They can come to therapy because their self-image is damaged, they just lost a relationship or an important job

• May be run down, in poor physical health

• When anxious, they can quickly swing to positive spin and back

• In conjoint sessions, Threes can demean others with a competitive style of delivery; positively reframe their role in relationships

• Avoid introspection, but respond well to suggestions and tasks

• Their social support system is often weak, although they might report otherwise

• Substance use can quiet the anxiety caused by neglecting their internal experience. Threes often have the energy for stellar performance even if their substance use becomes problematic. Better than average at concealing their addictions.

Healthy Threes are able to tap their creativity and manifest what they want through a combination of visualizing, positive thinking and hard work. They are flexible, willing to share their abundant energy and value the people in their lives. Threes are generally optimistic and able to accomplish whatever goals they set for themselves.

When caught in their unhealthy pattern, Threes are self-serving and competitive, needing all attention to be directed to their accom-plishments – real or manufactured. They become dismissive, aggres-sive and cutting towards whoever obstructs their positive self-image.

Superficial image management is an overlying goal of American consumer culture. Threes say that their false self is supported by the culture, so much so that it is difficult to feel motivated to change; some even said they needed to go elsewhere to be free of the constant reinforcement. Threes from other countries have mentioned that their personality style feels less unique here. American therapists could also have blind spots about what needs to change when working with Threes.

Childhood Experiences and Adult Defenses

Threes are usually energetic and creative children, earnestly meet-ing the world. They are keenly observant of their parents and authority figures and are sensitive to family definitions of success and failure. Recognizing what gets rewarded and approved of by "important" others comes naturally and the Three child may begin to sell what others will buy. Their accomplishments draw so much positive atten-tion that Three children begin to think their self-worth comes from an external source. They learn to place their faith in their ability to achieve.

When the truth of the Three child's inner experience threatens their external success, they unconsciously choose success. Their grow-ing anxiety over how they internally feel versus what the outer world expects of them is assuaged by a compulsion to keep succeeding: "I wanted my family's approval. My accomplishments made them proud. I made us all look good. I became my accomplishments."

Many Threes report having busy childhoods and some can pro-duce scrapbooks that document their early successes. A Three client may describe others in their family with an enthusiastic, positive spin recounting their special qualities and successes. However, they usually remember a milieu in which feelings weren't recognized and success was over-valued.

A Three's Genogram will often indicate a family role of "bright star" with lots of success and positive reinforcement. Many Threes played a precocious family role from the beginning, perhaps prompted by circumstances: the child went to work at an early age or stood out compared to other family members. For other Threes, this role devel-oped outside of the family.

The Three child learns to "become" an image of success by utilizing the defense mechanism of *identification* – unconsciously adopting the personality characteristics of others whom the Three envies or admires. Threes identify with a winning image to keep their inner experience from threatening their outer persona: "I had to identify with what it meant to be successful, otherwise you are a 'nobody', and no one wants to be nothing, especially in our family. So I joined the Foreign Service because it was my mother's idea of success. I was most wrong in what I was doing, but didn't give it up because that would have been failure. Instead I got double promotions!"

What Brings Threes to Therapy

Threes focus on the positive and screen out or discount negative feedback. This plus the fact that the culture amply rewards them for their achievement-oriented drive makes their seeking therapy unlikely unless a major crisis provokes it. A serious external blow to their self-image, caused by a job, relationship or status loss needs to occur before a Three will seek help. Interrupting drug and alcohol abuse or other compulsive behaviors can also precipitate such a crisis. A breakdown in health is another commonly reported cause for a Three to slow down enough to feel and reflect. As one Three who sought therapy said, "I saw myself flat on my back talking on my cell phone."

When a Three's activity slows, feelings they have repressed may surface, offering a golden opportunity for inner work: "In younger days when I was achieving, it was all about tasks; I got tremendous support for being successful. I got sick in my early forties, my immune system gave me problems first. I did not slow down or listen to my body at that time. In my mid forties I had to have major surgery and slow down. I had to rest and I was in nature. I really got the meaning of life and that I had been missing it. My emotions began to thaw, and tears came every time I tried to speed up. Still, I think it took me twice as long to heal because I kept doing more than my body was ready for. I was just getting the message slowly that I needed to pay attention and listen to my body."

A number of Threes described what it is like to reach the point of seeking psychotherapy:

• "I needed to see through the façade. I was staying in my marriage because performers don't fail. When things fell apart, I realized success often has nothing to do with a person's character. I lost respect for a lot of people in business, and pulled away. I was spiritually lost; in our family, we just focused on success and material things. We became self-congratulatory and didn't talk about our feelings. I have had to learn to let in other people's feelings. I thought, there has to be more to life than this. I got into therapy, went back to my home church, and began to place my hope in something more."

• "When things get bad enough, performers want to be successful, right? So when you are stuck in a place where you are not successful you want to get out of it. Everything had come at me at once; both parents were dying of cancer, my brother almost died of a drug overdose. My family, which had always been close, was in a feud. My husband wanted a divorce and I could not get a job."

• "My type has the tremendous need to cling to that image of myself, or the way I want people to see me. It costs an enormous amount of energy to keep up that image, but I have the energy in abundance...until I totally break down. The moment I cannot keep up the image I am totally lost. The world comes to an end and I want to die! For the first time I understood that during the biggest part of my life I had been running after an image, an idea about me. During my midlife crisis I was fundamentally confronted with the choice to live my true self or my imagined self. That time I could not run anymore after my image. I was tired. I was finished with that image…. I made the choice for my true self."

Therapy can also provide a safe place to talk about feelings that are unacceptable in other social contexts: "I did not want to burden my friends with what was failing in my life. A therapist gets paid for that."

What Does Not Work

Although Threes responded generously to the survey, they had more to say about how therapy failed than how it succeeded. The Three's defense of successful image-making and their hidden vulnerability are evident in their transference. The Three client's surface invitation to the therapist is to alleviate his anxiety by garnering approval for his performance. Underneath, however, they need emotional safety rather than approval. Threes can also be quick to judge therapists as incompetent and unlikely to help.

Depending on the therapist's own shadow, they may countertransferentially respond with impatience and insensitivity. Or they might collude with the often tenacious superficiality of the client's defense.

Some therapists find it difficult to keep open hearts with clients who are self-referencing and competitive. Some Threes said therapists responded to their surface bravado, but failed to make therapy safe enough for them to drop their mask and reveal their vulnerabilities:

"Threes look strong, but they really need TLC and emotional support."
Despite appearances, it is easy to scare a Three client away. One woman said her husband verbally attacked her during a marriage counseling session: "I had to leave when the therapist offered no protection. It looked like I had no heart, but my heart was so hurt. That's why all the layers of protection were there.

"Compassion from the therapist would have helped, but the therapist saw me as confident and able to handle a lot. He did not have a good read on my internal landscape and the session was brutalizing. I walked out and did not go back." One Three cautioned: "Until a Three is ready to see through the farce of the image, being forced to do so can make them suicidal."

Many Threes reported therapists who never saw past their smoke screen of positivism and allowed their problems to go untouched:

• "I wish therapists understood that the motivation for me to be the most brilliant and successful client they've ever had is too great. I need to be discouraged from achieving the obedient and clever client status. Then I am doing therapy and am working at it like a workaholic."

• "I had to be constantly on guard to not impress the therapist. This took a lot of attention – I gave myself a 'C' grade."

• "I saw a therapist for a few sessions when things were at their worst. He was buying into all my stuff; he was impressed by me and my accomplishments. I lost respect and thought 'damn, I've fooled this person too.' I had to leave." The therapist's awareness of his or her own identification with the image might have helped avoid the pitfall of colluding with this Three's successful storyline.

Author David Daniels points out that Threes are the "brief therapy super stars" of the Enneagram. A chameleon-like response to others whose approval they seek is normal. Any motive the therapist has will likely be picked up and mirrored as the Three seeks to impress: "I can tell what the therapist wants, shift to please the therapist, and perform the tasks of therapy well." For this reason, "solution focused" techniques are likely to seem highly effective in the short term while significant changes are circumvented. According to most of the Threes I interviewed, offering suggestions, particularly assigning tasks, is to be avoided: "The biggest mistake a therapist can make is to key into my desire for a solution and then give me one."

Because of their mastery at managing appearances, it is especially difficult to know when a Three is defended in therapy. False feelings "done well" can be difficult to distinguish from authentic ones. One

Three reported, "I may be vulnerable, but I can act like it's no big deal. I also may *appear* vulnerable but not really be feeling it. When I'm most defended, I'm smiling, on top of everything, explaining how and why I'm in therapy. Even if a nerve gets hit and I cry a little, I'm quickly back in control."

A therapist's goals for therapy could conflict with a Three's defenses. One remembered his therapist trying to take him into childhood pain when he just wanted to work on improving his present life: "As I got into counseling more deeply, I concluded that I was there as part of my constant efforts to become 'perfect.' You, know, like working out in the health club constantly to have an excellent body, or dressing in a particular way or driving a particular car.

"Therapy seemed to me like an extension of that. I wanted to find the problems, correct them so I could be even more of a 'performer' rather than getting to the truth of my experience and developing more peace and acceptance. I realized I wanted the therapist to focus on what I asked for and not my childhood. It is like if I hire a business consultant to evaluate my accounting department, I don't want them to start working with the management team just because they see some issues there."

It is understandable that therapists often do not recognize depression in Threes, since it can be well hidden: "I have a lot of energy, depression is masked with high energy. I can show the world what it wants to see, and I do a lot of masking. I have masks to cover pain, vulnerability, dreams, desires, past wounds, and masks to manage intimacy in relationships." Asking a hypothetical question like, "How would you look if you were in pain?" can give a therapist some insight into the person behind the mask.

What Does Work

Threes consistently recommended that therapists probe and ask questions rather than settle for appearances: "Even in therapy, it is complicated for a therapist to break down the image. Therapy is like fishing. A big fish has taken the bait and will run with it. If you jerk back the line too quickly it will snap. Pull too fast and the Three can also identify with the fish that is already caught, the victim, and make this the image. So, you let the fish come and go until it gets tired, till the game is exposed for what is: Running after an image!

"What helps is when the therapist pulls in on the line, gently telling me that he/she does see through my image building. Threes who have a clear understanding of the workings of image in themselves, will give therapists the opportunity to ask directly: 'Is this image or reality?' That is confrontation enough. Once the Three can work with this distinction you can go to the core of the problem. The fundamental escape route has been uncovered and the quest for the truth is now the more interesting game."

Many Threes suggest a "peeling back" or "freeze frame" approach: "The therapist needs to peel the layers, like an onion-skin, to help me get down to what is real. I will start on the surface. If the therapist can acknowledge me being there, but be patient and kind, then she can call me on my image and rhetoric and take me to the depth of a particular issue. I can fool people and say the right things; I need a therapist who can stay with me as I work through each layer and not be diverted. Honest feedback from the therapist if it does not seem complete; ask, or suggest I just sit with this for a minute and keep asking. Because I have to really look good, and will give good answers for the first four or five questions. I hear what you're saying – you're saying _____; is there anything deeper? Give me time to go to my heart. If the therapist knows NLP it would help them observe accurately. It is a questioning down kind of process."

Other Threes added concrete tips to make the risks of therapy tolerable:

- "Boundaries really help, if I know what the rules are I can feel inside of them."
- "Having a clock where I can see it."
- "Even if I don't ask for information it helps for the therapist to give it. Also, knowing the rules and what is normal helps me feel safe."
- "Remember: we are egomaniacs who are incredibly insecure."

Honesty and Truth

Threes who reported meaningful positive therapy experiences generally felt encouraged and supported to find their genuine emotional truth. One Three client sought therapy because, "When I visualized the old woman I will be, I knew I would regret that I did not feel my own feelings while they were happening. I wanted to change this while I could." This image became an anchor that her therapist returned to whenever the client would impatiently complain that the therapeutic process was not "getting her anywhere." Staying with the inevitable void behind the Three's persona produces anxiety. To protect themselves from the seemingly pointless feelings that surface, they may ask impatient questions like "Where are we going with this?" or "What are our goals?"

One woman describes the disconnected experience of first encountering her emotions during group therapy: "I would try to help *other* people in the group attain their goals, and when people cried I wondered why. Usually I rationalized that their childhood was worse than mine. I didn't get that my feelings were frozen, yet I felt uncomfortable that I couldn't tap into any of them. I just assumed my childhood was great."

Listening for a Three client's unacknowledged feelings and feeding back your observations can help them stay focused on their inner process: "I always reacted to other people who said they fear destitution and loneliness. I wanted to help them not feel, until I realized their fear was my fear. My lie was that I had no fear. I realized my core belief was that no one could love me, all they cared about was what I could do. I had never accepted the belief. Sitting with it allowed me to release it." Another Three described a breakthrough at a workshop: "We made masks, to show who we were really, under our professional image. I got a lot of positive attention for the mask I first made. Then I realized the mask was another false image; I needed to make a mask for my mask."

If the therapist can evoke the Three's capacity to self-observe, their inherent honesty about their image-making will often emerge: "It is still a struggle not to fall back on the habit of defending an image. Now I recognize the deceit almost immediately, even while I am talking, I see it coming. I make the decision to stick to the truth even when it hurts." Many Threes echoed that telling the truth had become a high priority: "I won't do things for image anymore, my image has gone to hell. I have to tell the truth as I see it – it is like a compulsion for me."

When Threes start telling the truth it can change the way they relate to others: "When I feel myself getting into the performer mode again I realize I'm not really listening to the other person. I shift my attention to just listen, with no agenda. I have become more and more direct. I just say what I believe, with no time for games and spins. When I played the game more, I was good at making people like me by telling half-truths and spinning. Now I get immediately uncomfortable when I start to do it. I have learned the relief of being comfortable in my skin."

Another Three described the process of keeping himself honest: "Now I get uncomfortable when I start to play a role. My inner observer is an alarm going off, telling me that I am going to twist the truth and to make the story more exciting. When I begin to see myself go into overdrive, it takes discipline not to jump in. It is as if I deny myself something rightfully mine; however, it's the wise thing to do. But I have to ensure that I do not get overtired. Otherwise, I do not see the overdrive coming and go straight into it with all the negative results."

Being attached to goals interferes with being present, because you are already in the future, perhaps performing for an imaginary audience. Becoming aware of these different states of attention, and how they feel in the body, can also strengthen a Three's self-observer. Learning about the contrast between the experience of identification and competition versus being authentically present is also useful: "In therapy, truth is the most powerful thing. To have a place to say anything, to feel comfortable and to acquaint myself with how I feel and have an emotional response. It's like I have a compass. I know how I feel, and then I have the choice to share what I want to share with others in my life."

Threes said that being physically tense and deceiving themselves go hand in hand:

• "Being asked what I feel in my body helps me recognize the connection between tension and deceit. Feeling my body anchors my head and my gut."

• "Deceit causes stress in my head and turns into acidity in my gut."

• "Deceit is physical, my heart rate elevates, it's fight or flight, and I might launch into it. Noticing my physical warning signals allows me to be aware. I can then know that I feel backed into a corner and I'm feeling I have to perform. This gives me the choice to stay honest."

• "Bodywork that helps me connect my mind with my body is especially helpful."

• "Heart-centered meditations are also healing."

Threes also affirmed the importance of taking time to practice looking inside themselves:

• "Living life without being driven by image is a more peaceful existence. If I'm not sure what the truth is, I take the time to think, ask to get back to the person later with my answer. The answer always comes up from my feelings if I give it time and space."

• "Truth can be mercurial. What is true now may not be later. So in relating truthfully, I have to interrupt the tendency to plan. If I plan to say how I'm feeling, I feel it's not true anymore. To allow myself to be immediately connected to what I feel – that's what I want."

Building time for reflection and silence into the therapy hour is also important, especially when things are going "too well":

• "Talk therapy let me just rationalize."

• "During my psychoanalysis I talked a lot. I was surprised that others do not talk a lot or hardly talk! While I am talking a lot, falling over my words, I am doing my 'show.' I live my image. I am most defensive. I remember one time the psychologist got angry because he was writing his hands off. I was talking and talking and talking, because it sounded so good in my own ears. But was it the truth? I discovered that there was only little truth and much fantasy, so much so that untruth prevailed. Consequently to stop the 'overdrive' was a very good thing. Becoming silent and trying to say little. But, making sure all of it is true."

• "One time I just sat with the therapist and said nothing...it was important."

• "It was helpful when the therapist made me stop talking. To make me breathe deeply, and keep silent. Bring me down in my silent self. To do away with the outer mask and go deep inside. That is very painful, most of the time."

• "Therapy helps in learning to question myself, asking 'is this really true for me?' When I've avoided the truth, I've avoided the feelings that go with it and therapy is an opportunity to bring truth and my feelings together."

As therapy gets deeper, being gentle with the travail of not knowing and not performing in therapy is important: "I was encouraged to explore slowly when at the core, to just be present and honest."

• "Hypnotherapy was helpful. In hypnotherapy, I got the image of standing on the edge of a cliff, you know where you have been and you have no choice but to leap into the unknown, with no image attached. I realized that listening to my inner guide was the way I had to live the rest of my life. This meant I could let go of setting outside goals and attaining them as a way of life. My inner guide would steer me in the right directions, I just needed to listen."

Therapists also earn a Three client's trust by being honest themselves: "Honesty from the therapist is essential. This can be about small things as long as it is genuine." Another Three added, "The therapist who is honest about their human failing allows me to let go of my need to play a role. They are really a person; I can be too. One therapist had trouble with Threes, I could tell anyway but her honesty helped me. If the therapist can stay really centered and come from all their knowledge they demonstrate fearlessness and this gives me the courage to be fearless in my vulnerability."

It is a relief for Threes to realize that they are good enough without having to pretend: "The psychotherapist has to help me to discover that I have done a lot of good things that do not depend on my image. People have looked through the image already a long time ago. Some of them wonder why I am walking on the top of my feet. People will accept me for what I am, basically a good person. Letting the image go and being your true self makes you much happier and gives you energy for other things!"

A minority of Threes said that brief therapy using behavioral strategies was the most helpful. If a client expects therapy to produce specific changes and meet concrete goals, solution-focused methods, coaching or self-help workshops may work better than psycho-dynamic approaches.

Some Threes preferred psycho-educational experiences to therapy or found them important in setting the stage for future therapy. Several Threes once found value in EST or one of its offshoots. Popular in the 1970s, EST (Erhard Seminar Training) was an experiential program developed by Werner Erhard that used group confrontation and a variety of applied theoretical models to promote personal change. While EST was criticized as cult-like and sometimes damaging to participants, one Three I interviewed said it changed his life: "The first program was great, I was introduced to eastern philosophy and meditation, but the second training was really *amazing*. Now that I had learned about the present, I learned how to manifest what I wanted in the future, and I've been doing this successfully ever since." I asked him if the second part actually taught him to be a better Three? He laughed and said "yes." Another Three said: "I went to Actualization, an offshoot of EST. I learned to read people better and fine-tune my skills. I became more aware of my pattern, setting the stage to challenge it, but that came later. I learned the Enneagram there and initially loved being a Three."

Other Threes found that esoteric spiritual approaches were helpful. Several mentioned the "Ridhwan school," also known as the "Diamond Way." Originated by A.H. Almaas, the school offers a synthesis of spiritual wisdom teachings, analytic psychology and the Enneagram. One Three explained: "I learned to check in with myself following the teacher's mirroring my persona in a generalized way over time. I learned to notice the sensations in my legs and arms and gut. This helps me know what I'm feeling as well as confirms my intuitions."

Success and Failure

The competitive paradigm of success and failure is imbedded in the thinking of Americans and amplified in Threes. Threes want therapists be mindful of this when working with them: "Seeing through the meaning of failure and success is important. My concepts of failure and success have changed. The looking for love, of course, was learning to love myself, but I kept wanting to see my value reflected in other people.

"In my Three fixation, whenever I won an award, I was immediately thinking about what was next. A friend said, 'why don't you just revel in tonight and not start working on the future?' I felt like I'd been slapped. It was shocking to see how much I was not with the moment.

"A therapist could help a Three really look at success by asking questions like, 'What exactly is important about it to you?' 'What is the inner part, the feeling underneath success?'

"But, you need to look at failure, too. A Three can rationalize it and gloss over it. Going into the pain is an opportunity to grow. A Three needs to understand the value of having feelings to get this concept."

Threes often see through themselves after a clear failure. It can be devastating to realize how competition and striving to attain approval have actually backfired and caused rejection: "The hardest question to ask is 'who am I?' As opposed to who society wants me to be. Finding hope means accepting that there is a path and a real place for you in the world." Therapists need to be alert to the spiritual opportunities at such times: "If a therapist can convey that I am really OK and that I do not have to do it alone, then I can feel that enlightened heart that is home. Living there is not only safe, it is the only place that is safe." A Three's empathy and compassion can also deepen: "I've learned to be more accepting of others and feel empathy with those who are not always successful. I see that everyone has value."

Family of Origin Work

A Three's sense of being falsely valued usually has its roots in childhood and exploring family dynamics provides an opportunity to revise understandings acquired in their family of origin: "I see my father, a Three, now in his 90s, with awards all over his walls. I could have been him. I knew that either I deal with these issues now or they will deal with me later in life." As Threes get more in touch with their feelings they often feel angry and need to grieve over how their inner life was co-opted by performing for others.

Asking Threes where they have "placed their hope" can unearth childhood misunderstandings about what is required to be a worthwhile human being. Asking what Threes believed was expected of them can reveal a lot about their likely current pain: "Get me to the pain of not feeling seen or accepted." But, it is also important to keep them focused: "Don't let me get near my pain and then avoid it." "Keep me connected to the vulnerable inner child and don't accept any perform-ing." Accepting these feelings ultimately allows Threes to love them-selves, giving them the freedom to be authentic.

It takes courage to continue to deconstruct an idealized and socially sanctioned persona. A Three client may need to be supported and validated to resist reverting to old coping mechanisms. Change often occurs in the unfamiliar landscape of rejection and loss and Threes need hope that they can be valued for more than performance: "Hope is important. The therapist needs to say there is hope, to be specific, to verbalize it."

Support Systems and Group Resources

Many Threes mentioned that group contexts had been helpful. It can be a relief, for instance, to discover that they can be accepted, even when they are not dazzling others with their accomplishments: "I was in a group, I intended to break through the garbage. I was looking good, fooling everyone, including myself, when one man said 'you have everyone in this group fooled, but not me.' He promised he would stay as long as it took me to break through the image. It was the truth and in that moment there was complete and utter liberation. Someone loved me enough to want the real me to come through.

"The biggest fear is no one will be there for you if they see the weakness and you will be alone. And the reality is people often do disappear when you aren't strong, so the fear gets reinforced."

It's not unusual for Threes to be emotionally isolated. If a therapist anticipates difficult work, it can be good ask the Three if there is someone in their life they can turn to for help; or whether there is anyone they can talk to when they feel sadness or experience failure. Because the actual support system of Threes can be thin, a group can offer a safe haven. By taking the focus off the successful image, groups can support a Three's newly emerging effort at honesty, as well as providing a safe environment for being a person with feelings. It is helpful to get honest feedback from others. Hearing negative impres-sions can feel devastating, but over-coddling can prevent growth.

Despite the fact that Threes advise that therapists confront them, they also want us to be sensitive to their vulnerability to image-damage in a family or group setting. One male Three who had felt humiliated by a therapist's confrontation recommended that therapists give them a chance to save face: "Framing a question in a way that would allow me to have an answer would have helped."

Reclaiming Lost Aspects of Self

As Threes reclaim the unseen aspects of themselves, art, fantasies, journaling, metaphors and symbolism are all helpful: "Asking me to paint or draw an image of my emotions works well. Playing helps me get out of my head and into my heart and body; inner child work creates a safe space for me to remember and feel things."

Threes said that therapy also offered:

• "An opportunity to practice asking for what I needed."

• "Practice at noticing feelings. Journaling about them, raw and as uncensored as possible, is also helpful. I needed to know that I could change gradually. To allow my feelings, I've had to learn to be with myself and be awake to the richness of my true experience."

• "A nurturing and non-judgmental environment with no comparisons and no expectations."

Using the Enneagram

The Three client I mentioned who walked out of the marriage session also said: "If the therapist had understood the language of the Enneagram, he might have told my husband 'you are painting a picture that makes her look really bad, do you understand that her image is really important to her? Then he could have explained that image was protection for my heart. I felt it looked like I had no heart; by phrasing it in this way, I might have felt acknowledged and seen. The layers of protection and concern for how it looks are there because the heart is so hurt." The defense mechanisms and fixations mapped by the Enneagram are also a resource: "I am convinced that I would have benefited tremendously if I had been confronted with the characteristics and patterns of my type during the sessions."

Connecting Points
Three Connects to Six

The connections to Six and Nine both expand the Three's emotional range. However, the expression, 'things often get worse in therapy before they get better' appears especially true for Threes: "When feelings start to thaw, it's good, but it feels like a breakdown."

Getting in touch with the anxiety and self-doubt of the Six can be destabilizing to the usually confident Three. As uncomfortable as this is, questioning and self-doubt are good medicine, illuminating complexities and deeper truths. The therapist might also help the Three realize that the high-side qualities of Six, such as loyalty and intuition, are also more available and can be nurtured.

Three Connects to Nine

As a Three slows down and becomes less task and image oriented, their connection to Nine also starts to emerge. It helps Threes become more connected to their bodies and relinquish neurotic control. They are also more able to appreciate others and recognize them as important. Since a Three's habitual attention is focused on personal success, being unguardedly "in the moment" evokes anxieties and internal conflicts that can be usefully worked with.

The connection to Nine also helps Threes let go of successes, although this can create tension. Therapy can provide a place for Threes to more deeply clarify their values: "I feel like it's OK to just be human, to have not achieved all the possible goals one could achieve and be recognized for. I've realized that life is richer than accomplishment." As the compulsion to achieve softens, the down side of Nine – forgetting and avoiding tasks – may require that the Three develop a new balance between being and doing.

Dreams

Using dreams in therapy is another way for Threes to find deeper truths. The following dream helped the dreamer see her desire to be authentically recognized and valued: "The President was giving an important address about the state of the Nation. He was hyped over playing to the crowd. He did not seem to be the real thing. His wife walked into the room in the middle of his address. She is mortified she is late and embarrassing him. She does not have on any makeup, and is in blue jeans and a shirt. She goes to the back of the room. At the end of his address he brings her to the front of the room, puts his arm around her and introduces her. She has put on lipstick. They sit down to the side of the stage; he has tears in his eyes. He obviously has love, understanding, compassion, at her genuineness, lack of guile, her openness, lack of artifice, just being who she is."

Good Enough Therapy

The good enough therapist provides a Three client with a safe place to stop performing and a mirror in which to see their own authenticity: "It is a relief when someone sees through the image, if they can be there, you just want to let them see all the wounds and be held like a baby. It is like in the Velveteen Rabbit: when your fuzz rubs off, you can be real!"

In the treatment relationship, a Three is valued for being rather than doing. They learn to value being present to their true experience over a persona sold well. When they let go of the need to compete, to be the best in someone else's eyes, they find their true individuality and personal truth.

Fours

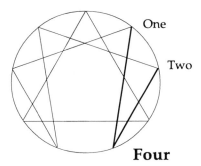

Presentation in Therapy

- Fours can present themselves as outsiders
- Some are moody, introspective, or quietly reserved; others have a dramatic artistic style
- They may want help with depression and unresolved grief
- Can have low self-esteem and feelings of being flawed
- They can be angry, provocative or intentionally shocking
- They often search for the authentic, while resisting the ordinary; may have trouble with structuring daily life
- Distorted body image and a sense of flaw can support eating disorders
- Fours who abuse substances often operate from a romanticized, self-destructive image of an "artist-addict." If they are attached to this identity it can thwart their efforts at sobriety. Substance abuse also increases depression and distorts reality, fueling dangerous fantasies and risky behavior.

Healthy Fours are attuned to the beauty, creative spirit, depth and paradoxes of existence. At their best, they naturally balance the material and spiritual parts of life and allow themselves to be both productive and happy.

When caught in the down side of their personality pattern, Fours can be consumed with what is wrong with themselves, even shamefully withdrawing into despair and depression. They can also split in the direction of believing they are more special than others and not therefore subject to ordinary expectations, over-dramatizing their life as separate from and more difficult than others.

The Four's attention style is often drawn toward what is missing. They are attracted to depth and are willing to stay with sadness and the darker side of life. Depending on the individual, this can be authentic or more about image. Fours are attracted to what they perceive to be genuine. Many have a distinctive, graceful and artistic manner.

The Four persona represents both idealized and devalued aspects of American culture. Idealized themes that promote a romantic, dramatic life over an ordinary one are reflected in arts, popular music and Hollywood fantasies. Photographs, songs and books about charismatic yet tragic figures like James Dean, Elvis Presley, Marilyn Monroe and Jim Morrison continue to sell years after their deaths. However, a task and accomplishment-driven culture does not readily value people who search for life's deeper meanings and embrace a poetic aesthetic style.

Fours, especially as adolescents, can strongly identify with romantic ideals, yet feel badly for being out-of-step with cultural norms. This conflict sometimes exaggerates a Four's sense of being both special and flawed. It also intensifies their tendency to inhabit exotic fantasies instead of ordinary reality.

Childhood Experiences and Adult Defenses

Fours are inherently gifted with a conscious connection to their unconscious mind, giving them a deep creativity and the ability to recognize the sacred in the ordinary. They also feel loved and accepted and feel they have a unique essential place in the world.

As children, however, Fours often feel abandoned and when Four clients relate their history they usually describe a pattern of loss. They often remember being especially cherished and then rejected or deserted. As the Four child tries to make meaning of this experience, they develop a self-image of someone flawed. To compensate they imagine they are special and unique in ways that no one else can understand. This strategy allows the child to separate him or herself from others – who are seen as ordinary and mundane – and yet belong to life in a way the others cannot.

This sets up a pattern of envy and longing. Fours avoid a painful present by imagining what will be in the future or could have been in the past – both of which are unavailable now. Rich, seductive and compelling, a Four's fantasy life is soothing. To maintain it, though, the Four has to push other people away. When the Four is in this emotional state, the efforts of others to connect interrupts the pleasure of their private longing and makes the Four feel vulnerable to more abandonment.

The Four child usually appears sensitive, creative, and unique. Some can seem overtly troubled, either provocative and angry or contained and removed. One Four described her teen years: "In my family, the intensity of my inner experience was not encouraged. I learned over time to keep my feelings quiet and hold to task, to live a very exterior life. Unfortunately, that makes me feel invisible and sometimes a bit schizophrenic, as I have a very different inner experience from my outer one."

Another Four told of his family's reaction to him and his response: "As a kid my show of unhappiness engaged the adults, the attention felt good, but then I felt I was seen as broken, which made me ashamed." People in the Four's life may take the hint and distance themselves emotionally because of the Four's "come close – go away" messages. This apparent rejection then reinforces the Four's feeling of being an outsider. Because Fours are likely to absorb, and sometimes act out, the taboos and emotional blind spots of the family system, they often become the family scapegoat.

A Four's envy and longing are supported by the defense mechanism of introjection, the symbolic taking into the self of a loved or hated person or external object – the converse of projection. It is easy to understand how a positive introjection would protect a Four, but introjecting a negative person or object seems paradoxical. One Four explained how the defense worked for him: "I walk through the coffee house and four people I know greet me warmly, but I perceive one person as rejecting. I focus on that person and it changes my whole experience of myself. I absorb all the negative energy in the room and feel those feelings while I'm meeting my friend for coffee. This helps me stay stuck and comfortable, and gives me an excuse not to take risks. When I get this way, longing for an unavailable relationship is safer than having a relationship with a real and available person." Thus, the negative introject gives psychological protection from potential abandonment, while maintaining an isolation in which longing and envy can thrive.

What Brings Fours to Therapy

Because Fours don't fit easily into the status quo, their inner experience is often incongruent with what they believe is outwardly "normal." This reinforces their sense of being flawed: "Low self-esteem is behind my seeking therapy. I need to be recognized by the therapist as special, not more special than others, just as having something unique to contribute to the world." The promise of being understood and seen as special may draw Fours towards a therapeutic relationship. "I like feeling understood," as one put it, "it's so rare."

What Does Not Work

Fours reported two common mistakes by therapists: (1) offering interpretations too quickly, leaving the Four client feeling unseen or judged, and (2) becoming over-involved with the Four client's interesting introspective storyline while missing the client's underlying issues.

Several Fours recalled therapists who seemed impatient and didn't listen long enough before offering solutions: "There are things I would like to have experienced more of in therapy. Naturally they are the things I would like to have experienced in my family of origin. I would like to have had my feelings, experiences and perceptions validated before being told what I could do differently. I find it hard to be open to advice if I don't feel validated first. I would have liked to have more positive feedback."

Some Fours said therapists had seemed uncomfortable with their emotional sensitivity and intervened too quickly, reinforcing the Four's sense of alienation: "I think that therapists need to understand that Fours are pretty sensitive, so they need to be maybe a little more sensitive than usual in working with us. Good advice would be: Don't rush in to try the latest clever technique for a quick fix; just listen for a while, until you are pretty sure you understand. I've been quite turned off when therapists have made personal statements about me in harsh or critical language, lacking in empathy and pointing out my weaknesses as though I was a bad person."

Another common mistake therapists made was to prematurely normalize and contextualize the Four client's feelings of being an "alienated outsider." The client usually reacted with disdain for the therapist and shame at themselves for being so hard to understand. Therapeutic approaches limited to prescribing 'healthy' new behavior or cognitive change were generally considered too superficial: "Marriage therapists just stayed on the surface, had him bring me flowers. The real issues were never touched."

Therapists can also get caught in helping Four clients process their emotions and dramas while forgetting to help the client change. Although it can seem compelling, focusing on ever-more-interesting memories, traumas and introspective analysis can feed the client's false self. Although Fours sometimes court this response, if the therapist falls for it, the client may ultimately feel unseen: "Don't be impressed with my depth and creativity," one Four explained, "Ask me what's going on underneath."

Because Fours seem to both romanticize and avoid their own shadow, discerning how they really feel is sometimes difficult. A therapist could over-engage a Four client's image or become impatient and prematurely interrupt an important moment of processing. While Fours want to be understood, they also fear being exposed and judged. To protect themselves, they can create distance by being remote, obscure or dramatic; unconsciously rejecting any effort others make to understand them. The paradox, of course, is that while the Four cannot be exposed and judged, she cannot be truly understood either.

This pattern is sometimes acted out in the treatment relationship. A therapist could give the Four client well-timed honest feedback about what it feels like to be drawn in and then pushed away. The client might then see their role in creating disappointments in their relationships, identify their internal motives and make conscious changes.

In the transference / counter-transference relationship the therapist may feel special or devalued or both. Disappointed, melancholic Four clients can implicitly entreat the therapist to be overly helpful, creating a fruitless rescue drama.

Fours say that when they feel defended in therapy they may intellectualize, quietly withdraw, be emotionally intense, verbally cutting or project an air of superiority:

- "I tend to go very internal, get very quiet and emotionally turn to stone. Inside it feels like a form of shock, but outside it probably looks like withholding, withdrawing out of anger perhaps. After I figure out how to respond (which might be an overly calm thing or might be quite emotional) and then get through the response, I often get shaky, cry a lot. My choice would be to be private and pretty isolated at that time, so I don't have to show it."
- "I show disdain and contempt, and feel I know more about emotions than the therapist. When I do this I am compensating for not being normal and not fitting in. This is a good indication of terror."

- "Talking about feelings can be a way to not feel them."
- "I'm most defended when I feel someone has not accepted or liked me. I take much to a personal level that does not belong there."

What Does Work

Fours emphasized that they need to feel safe in the therapy relationship: "Basic safety comes first, finding out if the therapist is not going to abandon or judge me. This can take a long time, and there are moments when you don't believe you are safe, regardless of the therapist's positive history."

Several Fours valued therapists who were authentic: "It's more the psychological health of the therapist, their emotional availability and their willingness to acknowledge any mistake they might make that is helpful for me. I don't think it has been any one therapeutic modality that has been of benefit. I think what's important is the relationship that develops between therapist and client, the sense of trust, lack of judgment, validation of feelings, good boundaries, professionalism and the elusive chemistry. It's also important for me to feel that the therapist really likes me and is genuinely interested in my well being."

Another Four wanted to be certain a therapist could skillfully take her to the depths she needed: "When I go to therapy it's not for minor stuff. It's as if I'm afraid of heights and to deal with that I'm going to have to look over the rim of the Grand Canyon. If the therapist says, "okay, let's look," I'm going to panic, want to talk about why I'm afraid of heights, and how it feels to be afraid of heights, and aren't those gorgeous clouds, etc. So if they say, let's start by looking over this four-foot drop, and when you can do that we'll go on, that helps me. And if they get to ten-foot drops and stay there – doing the same depth over and over – I'll get bored. I do want to get to the heart of the matter, to change the core, and I'm also terrified the core will be awful and the therapist will leave. I need to trust the therapist big time and not be pushed too hard at first."

Fours can be intellectual, but they basically process life through their emotions: "When I have dealt with fact collectors and theoreticians I have felt at a disadvantage, because my beliefs do stem from my feelings, not my head. I'm not even that good at retaining factual information, but I strongly hold the feelings of the information I have gathered. I'm sort of a sieve for facts but a steel trap for emotional information. It really helps me if the counselor with whom I'm working has earned my trust by truly seeming to understand the intensity and sometimes weirdness of my operation from such a feeling place. At times my therapist responded to something I said from such a heart place that it jolted me into really getting what had happened."

A therapist may need to see past the Four's articulate self-insightful persona in order to work with the underlying issues: "I am pretty capable verbally, but I can bury my interior, vulnerable self. By the time I ask for help I may sound like I know exactly what my problem is and what I need, but I can't truly get in touch with it. I think as a Four I've been taught not to display that inner self and so I need to feel really heard on a deep level. I need a therapist who can help me put words on my real feelings and help me know those feelings are all right, thereby earning my trust. Being misperceived and being labeled as too intense for a lot of years has trained me to hide myself, and I do a sort of jump out jump back thing with exposing myself. If I move into that place where I simply don't share my inner self, I then feel like I've disappeared and this fake person is presenting herself and everyone is buying it. Then I feel misunderstood, and that's the special/flawed place."

For therapists, understanding shame is essential and this is a particularly delicate area for Fours. In difficult moments, Four clients recommended that the therapist offer a balance of therapeutic silence and careful interpretation: "Most helpful is when someone I trust can just sit with me through the defense, not try to talk me out of the place I'm in but maybe help me attach words to my feelings. Time helps me a lot, gives me perspective and allows me to experience the situation from the other point of view. It is good for me to not wait too long, though, because I sometimes misplace my energy by endlessly re-playing the situation in my mind."

Therapy helps Fours learn to observe themselves and make conscious choices: "After about six months in therapy I began to "hear" the critical voice in my head and realize how I set myself up." Some Fours said that no particular therapeutic method worked best; instead they credited empathetic and skillful therapeutic direction: "A whole variety of standard therapy "tricks" to help clients get in touch with their feelings can be helpful, such as laughing with me over my big words, or asking me how I feel, or using a Gestalt technique or gentle curiosity followed by simple but genuine empathic understanding."

Getting Grounded

When Four clients engage in cycles of longing, envy, and fantasy, it is better to help them get grounded in the present before plumbing new emotional depths. Shame and pain may overwhelm Fours at various points and using insight therapy alone can actually intensify their defensive longing. External activities like gardening, cooking, childcare, eldercare and practices of a practical, earthy nature can help. During one of our Enneagram Four panels, all of the participants said that they had worked in nursing homes during their late teens and early twenties. Serving vulnerable people took them out of themselves and gave them a perspective on their own lives at a time they needed it most.

When Fours fail to fulfill their ordinary life commitments, they damage their relationships, causing themselves more losses and reinforcing their shame: "For me I have to make a conscious effort to function in the mundane life; there is hatred of tasks, but I have to remember I feel better when my life is in order. I also have empathy for how others are affected when I don't do the ordinary things." Ungrounded fantasies and imagination can seduce Fours away from real life; using intoxicants and substances can increase the danger of dramatic, self-destructive behavior: "I'm aware that on the lower side of my type, I have difficulty finding contentment with the present. My longing is for more and deeper experiences, which keeps me from seeing the beauty in the now. A therapist should help me stay with the mundane."

When Fours are in recovery from addictions, learning to find value in the ordinary is particularly important. It is enticing to retreat into fantasy and longing when painful realities are no longer medicated. Four addicts usually have to work through feelings of envy for others who use substances without problems or consequence. The Four's "flaw" complex is especially important to recognize and work with to avoid relapse.

One Four said that in the early stages of therapy she expected her therapist to prove that she – the client – was special, by seeking her out and rescuing her. Her therapist's healthy boundaries helped: "A couple of times I quit and waited to see if she would call and beg me to return to therapy. Then I realized she wouldn't, it was up to me, the relationship wouldn't save me."

A Four client may need different things from therapy at different life stages. A 28-year-old Four said: "As a child I was angry, had horrible rages. Being sent to a counselor reinforced my sense of flaw. I was not open to it. I see the same counselor now, however, and she is wonderful." A period of supportive talk therapy could be just right for a teenager who needs to experience trust and feel listened to by someone. More intense work may be too scary or disruptive. As a foundation for future therapy, a therapist might consider communicating to their Four clients a message like: "I'm not minimizing the importance of processing deeper issues, but developing some practical coping skills first is going to make that safer and easier."

Working with Introjection and Shame

One Four described the interplay between his flawed image and the part of himself he believed was special: "I would be suicidal when I was an adolescent and all my energy would go into making things worse because I was so hypnotized by the dark side. But, I also had fantasies of being rescued by some 'other' who recognized me as special." When Fours are caught in this kind of depressive vortex they give the locus of control to imaginary others. Unless the Four learns that only they can rescue themselves, they will stay stuck. The Four quoted above recommended that therapists encourage clients like him to learn to deliberately use introjection to internalize positive experiences and qualities. Sources might be in nature, beautiful music, art or whatever is healthy and meaningful for the individual. Another Four explained: "I learned to be in beautiful places and to ask for help. Each time I did, I found I was given what I needed."

One Four said her therapist helped her overcome her negative introjection and shame by giving her affirming messages during hypnosis: *"There is nothing you need to change about yourself..... You are exactly the person you should be .....you are beginning to live the life you were supposed to have."*

Fours also need to learn that comparing themselves to others exaggerates their flawed/special complex. A therapist's well-timed self-disclosure could reassure a Four client that we are all flawed and share a common humanity: "I idealize therapists as having it all together, but when my therapist shared something about his history I felt less shame for being who I was."

Several Fours mentioned that their shame initially blocked the therapist's feedback: "I needed to learn to accept feedback. While painful, working with imagery helps because it takes me back to feel the sadness or pain, even though I don't want to go, and then I describe it to my therapist. It is also contained, I'm feeling pain only as much as I can tolerate. It gives me insights into patterns and how different people responded to me, and the role I played. I can accept this and have less shame, and take the insights I've gained back to my relationship with my boyfriend."

Longing and Creative Connection

Fours fear that without the defensive distance that longing creates, their authentic self will be vulnerable to certain rejection: "I have a real fear of being myself, like I will be abandoned if I am myself."

When moving into deeper work with Fours, listen for how they experience their connection to their own creativity. When they experience art, music, nature, or beauty, what feelings and insights come to them? Through this connection Fours often feel their most authentic and alive, but they may need to learn that the connection is intuitive and within them and will therefore not abandon them. The therapist can help integrate this insight as the work proceeds. It will help counteract the Four's neurotic belief that they must be lacking something.

Here a Four describes childhood experiences that helped her cope: "As a child I had asthma and my mom would act as if I was doing it on purpose. For me I had to feel that abandonment in psychotherapy, to float around in it, and remember the threads that actually got me out of it. I loved art, swimming, the soothing floating feeling of being held by water, playing in the sandbox for hours, just feeling the sand. All of these helped me know there was a bigger picture."

Mind/Body and Right Brain Approaches

Some Fours recommended disciplines that integrate the body. Speaking of Hakomi, this woman said: "Art therapy gave me big insights into how I resist feedback or help from others. But only a body centered approach broke through." Methods that access the creative "right brain" helped other Fours get past their intellectual defenses: "I got a lot out of visualizations with my eyes shut. I didn't have time to figure out the 'correct' answer but rather went to my first impression. This got me to some true broken-free places that I could then move on from. I also felt met and held rather than watched or judged. I think I need permission to get a tiny bit comfortable with being anything even approaching needy. So this really helped me."

When their symptoms did not respond to cognitive approaches, some Four clients found value in techniques designed to access unconscious or dissociated content: "Guided imagery takes me out of my rational mental mind and gets me into my feelings." They also recommended EMDR and Brain Gym techniques.

To alter their grief and shame, other Fours suggested using Gestalt therapy's "empty chair" technique as well as working with dreams and metaphors. Also useful were creative efforts, using painting, writing, music, and dance. Telling a story of childhood through painting or poetry, for instance, could give a Four a sense of mastery over their remembered emotions.

Using Symbols

Using symbols with Fours can have a profound impact. Like poetry and dreams they bypass intellectual defense: "When I met my therapist she had the Chinese character for crisis in her office and she explained to me it meant 'Opportunity on rough water.' I needed to talk about symbolism, I had been analyzing the hell out of myself, reading books and trying to make meaning. Figuring out who I was, seeing my anger and judgment, seeing that everyone has problems, that most people are doing the best they can – all this helped me normalize my experience. Learning to find a framework for my sensitivity and learning to have boundaries around my empathy also helped."

Working With Melancholia and Depression

Understanding the difference between melancholia and depression is important when working with Fours. Being attracted to the dark side of life is not grounds alone for treatment and many Fours would agree with this client's statement: "Grief and sadness are part of my identity."

Several Fours recommended that therapists ask detailed questions to distinguish between their experience of melancholia and depression. While the two inner states may look similar from the outside, Fours can find melancholia creatively stimulating, but actively avoid depression: "Depression is such a scary place because it seems static, it won't move. I'm trying to keep the emotions from happening. Fighting it is exhausting."

Most mature Fours have experienced enough depression to suggest ways to avoid or lessen it:

• "My fear when I get depressed is that it will never end. I will have to stay stuck in it. Over time, though I've learned that it eventually changes."

• "Knowing I have the conscious ability to engage it and it will dissipate allows me freedom. If I let it happen consciously it will move. Helpful were meditations of being in the 'awful moment' memory, and sitting through the feeling until it transforms."

• "I refuse to be uninformed but I have to watch for depression when I am becoming 'over-informed.'"

• "I need to screen out aspects of life that might take me over the edge and into a depression that is hard to get back out of. It helps to limit negative information and people, turn off the news, and realize I have a choice. For example, journaling is helpful, but too much journaling and introversion is not helpful. I need to balance extroversion and introversion."

Many Fours said they learned to counterbalance past losses by focusing on their present resources: "Knowing there are strategies and options that can help. Calling people, doing tasks, asking for help and learning who to trust have all been valuable." Several Fours also recommended St. John's Wort as an anti-depressant, perhaps in part because it is unconventional and out of the mainstream.

Emotionality Versus Authenticity

When Fours avoid feelings they fear will lead to depression, they start to defensively distance themselves from all their feelings. Meanwhile they may hide behind an image of emotional sensitivity. "I have a romance with emotionality," one Four explained, "but I am really reluctant to go into my true emotions. I can cry for the state of the world but the personal is not so easy to know even for me. If I was authentic regarding my own pain I would let others down because I wouldn't be who they want me to be. The drama of my emotionality is a paradox, a smoke screen to keep anyone from really getting close to my true feelings."

Longing Versus Letting Go

Enneagram author Richard Rohr described Fours as "refusing to mourn." Since they can be attached to longing for a lost object or person, Fours can find it especially difficult to let go when it's really necessary, i.e. when someone has left. Allowing themselves to meet a feeling of loss at its root and effectively grieve it can be a challenge. To create motivation and help Four clients realize they have a choice, therapists can guide them to visualize their future – what will happen if they hang on versus what will happen if they let go.

In the face of a Four's chronic longing, therapists may also have to be firm. A generally well-balanced Four client of mine became caught in a damaging cycle of grief, rage, re-attachment and despair as she went through a tumultuous divorce. The marriage always held hope from a distance, yet she was extremely unhappy when in it. As her therapist I was increasingly concerned about her worsening condition and strongly confronted her about the destructive drama she was acting out. She agreed to do a marathon of journaling and soul searching. She began to grieve the loss of her marriage and experienced significant emotional release. Later, she joked about wanting to create a bumper sticker that read: "Life has been better since I gave up hope." Staying attached to what could have been robs the Four of the richness of what is.

Connecting to a Creative Source

Since Fours are often sensitive to the symbolic and artistic, making use of pertinent poetry, literature and movies can be exceptionally beneficial. I treated a gifted young Four in the grip of a major depression. She was dangerously suicidal and would bring me depressive poems by Sylvia Plath and others. I found poems and literary references to share with her; all of them made a case for living. Sometimes this felt like "dueling poetry." Thankfully, my poets seemed to help her survive the worst of her depression.

Mary Oliver's poem, "Members of the Tribe," seemed most powerful in countering my client's despair. In this eloquent poem Oliver speaks of artists and poets who choose death, of forgiving their despair and even their choice, but not forgiving how they lead others to death "with their exquisite poems. Ahead of me they were lighting their fires in the dark forests of death." Oliver goes on to affirm the value of work and ordinary life: "And the man who merely washed Michelangelo's brushes, kneeling – on the damp bricks, staring – every day at the colors pouring out of them, lived to be a hundred years old." (*Dream Work*, pg 32.)

Finding Balance

Several Fours found value in experiencing their darker emotions, as long as they maintained their balance: "It's good for a therapist to make things really meaningful for Fours. I'm having a hard time right now, but I know something good is going to come out of it, a magical creative depth." It is also helpful, however, for Fours to realize that there are other ways to grow: "I was happy to find tools that helped me *not* react to every intense feeling I have."

Another Four adds: "Therapy helped me develop the ability to observe myself. I could tell my therapist what happened and why I thought I did things. She shared her observations and validated my feelings of aloneness. Essentially she said, 'you are different and it is a double-edged sword.' She acknowledged that it was rough and lonely, but she would also stop me if I started feeling sorry for myself. She would remind me of my gifts, and make me recognize I had no business feeling self-pity."

Relationship Work

When they unconsciously replicate childhood dynamics in their present relationships, Fours usually set themselves up to feel alone and abandoned. Their push-pull approach to intimacy, as well as their emotional intensity, can confuse and frustrate partners and family members. Paradoxically, their fear of being abandoned can prompt a Four to act sarcastic, outrageous and dramatic in ways that shock. If a client behaves this way, it's good to focus on what he or she intends by the behavior or is feeling underneath it; this will often reveal deeper issues and genuine pain. If a Four's underlying feelings are validated they may feel safe enough to look at their behavior from other people's points of view. They may then agree that they create the abandonment they fear.

One Four said that role-playing helped her recognize how her criticality was damaging her relationship: "During couples therapy the therapist had my boyfriend stand with his back to me. Then she had me stand behind him and shake my finger at him. I suddenly saw what I was doing, I saw myself shaming him and I sobbed as I realized how I was capable of being so hurtful to someone. The relationship later ended but I saw myself more honestly."

The Four also realized she was replaying a childhood dynamic with her father, whom she could never please. This time, however, she was the powerful parent, rather than the helpless child. When the therapist had the couple reverse roles, she was able to grieve for herself: "From the child's position I was crying, no one understood me. I didn't feel I could get what I wanted."

A Four's intensity can cause others, including therapists, to minimize their legitimate issues. Since they can be nonconformist and unconventional, they are often seen as identified patients. Therapists doing family work should take care not to side too quickly with a Four's calm, reasonable partner or family member.

Connecting Points
Four Connects to One

Fours have a connection to One and Two, both of which help them balance their inner life and engage with others. The high side of the connection to One helps Fours focus on the present and take positive, practical action. This is an antidote to their dysfunctional angst, especially around completing the basic tasks of life. The connection to One can also give Fours a vision of fairness, social justice and a desire to make the world better. On the down side, the Four's connection to One can amplify their shame and criticality.

Four Connects to Two

The Four's connection to Two brings them out of their self-absorbed isolation. They often become empathetic and generous towards others.

On the low side, however, Fours can over-give in an effort to be special. Meanwhile they neglect their own needs, much like an unhealthy Two: "Sometimes I hung in too long with therapy I knew was not good for me. Even though bad, it was attention, and I feel like I have to take care of other people." Two-like seductive caring combined with the Four's pushing-away behavior can confuse relationships: "In college, my friends told me I could be so 'there' for others – and then so cruel, selfish and uncaring. It was about keeping distance."

Dreams

Several Fours mentioned that dream work had been beneficial: "I worked with my dreams with a Jungian therapist. This symbolic work was very useful to me. She had a wonderful way of being supportive and connected and asking questions about my dreams that left me feeling confronted by myself, and not by her. She described the dreams as being like personalized ink blots. I liked that. At the end of our work together I had a dream about looking at my psyche on a psychological print out and seeing the highs and lows and accepting my differences from the norm in the same way that we all have highs and lows and differences from the norm. I still think of that as a good lesson I realized in therapy."

Another Four said: "… dream work has been my tool to connect with my deepest self and in listening to my dreams, I have learned to not judge myself as harshly and see my connection with others. It has been my 'cure' for depression, my need for the sacred in life, sense of wonder, drama and creativity."

Dreams of being naked in public are universal. However, in a uniquely Four variation, a woman recounted the following repetitive dream: "I am somewhere, usually inside a house or building. I'm naked, and happy to be so. I need to go somewhere and as I pass people they are horrified to see me naked. Sometimes I feel sorry for them early on and put something on or try to cover myself a little, but in most of the dreams I am defiant for quite a while, torqued that they can't cope with nudity.

"After a while I give in and put on a shirt or partial cover. I never dress fully, but enough to make it easier on them. I remain irritated that they're so traumatized by the sight of me, usually thinking, 'grow up, get over it, for heaven's sake.' And I feel stressed, having to wear things to keep them happy, to keep them calm. I want to get to a place where I can uncover again, where I can breathe."

Good Enough Therapy

The good enough therapist accepts the Four for who they are by listening and understanding without judging. The masks that protect the Four from authentic presence can be exposed if the client is ready and the relationship provides enough safety and skillful means. Therapy must ultimately help Four clients realize that they have abandoned themselves and that the relationship to the beloved that they seek in others can only be found within. Getting Four clients connected to their genuine emotions and encouraging/supporting any necessary grieving can free them from dysfunctional longing and drama. When the suffering created by envy is effectively worked with it changes into its opposite – equanimity. When Fours understand that what they long for is their own essential self, they can become happy.

Fives

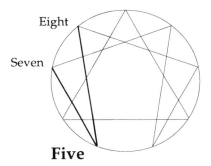

Eight

Seven

Five

Presentation in Therapy
- Five clients may be shy and guarded with a flat affect
- They may offer brief responses or intellectual verbosity
- Can act superior, over-intellectualize and avoid feelings
- Loneliness is often a motivator
- Some Fives come to therapy to understand how emotional and social systems function. They may be brought in by a spouse who wants better communication
- Fives can appear anxious, scanning, afraid of exposure or intrusion
- Some Fives seem innocent of social conventions and openly answer questions about subjects usually loaded with social secrecy: eating disorders, substance abuse, and sexual or other compulsions
- Fives can abuse substances to relieve social anxiety, using alcohol and/or drugs to numb and quiet their fear.

At their best Fives are engaged in their own life through their relationships and work. Doing what they feel passionate about, they are willing to give of their time, knowledge and emotions.

When Fives are caught in their defensive pattern, they get trapped in loneliness. They avoid having to give to or be touched by others and hoard what they have acquired. Their attention is geared toward maintaining privacy and observing the external world. They spend a lot of time gathering information, which seems to provide them safety by allowing them to know more than others.

The Five introspective style is out of sync with the aggressive, busy, forward-moving aspects of American culture. The Five's mental acuity – while a strength – can set them apart socially and their other gifts may be overlooked and undervalued. The marketing of "Social Anxiety Disorder" by the pharmaceutical industry reflects this bias. This trend encourages clinicians to diagnose normal children who have the characteristics of Fives and give them medication to become more extroverted.

Childhood Experiences and Adult Defenses

Fives have the inherent gift of omniscience, an intuitive intelligence and wisdom that is not intellectual. They are also naturally able to be fully present without becoming attached to outcome. These essential qualities underlie the kind of presence and compassion taught by the Buddha.

As children, however, Fives can experience the world as overwhelming, intrusive or unreliable. Five children are sensitive to other people's emotional states and often come to believe that others will not meet their needs without wanting too much in return. To protect themselves from feeling depleted, young Fives learn to tamp down their life force. This allows them to need less from others, thus minimizing their risk should nothing be available. The Five child begins to habitually guard his privacy as well as gather and hoard information, an early expression of what Enneagram books call avarice, or greed.

Some Fives remember childhoods where they felt intruded upon, perhaps because of a crowded family environment or because of needy or demanding parents. Other Fives were paid little attention and recall an atmosphere of emotional scarcity. Either experience prompts the child to hold on to what little they feel they have. Most Fives remember feeling comforted by time alone, when they often read books or played with computers to mentally escape. Social rules were also a source of confusion and loneliness, further prompting the Five child to withdraw: "As a child, I took a very detached role in the family. Doing my own thing. It's as if I made a decision very early in life that it was safer to do without intimate relationships."

From the outside Fives appear self-contained and undemanding; even as children they may not seem to need much. So it is easy to understand how unintentional neglect could materialize: "My mother was unavailable to me as a young child because a disabling condition made it difficult for her to care for three young children. She told me once that she thought she neglected me the most because I was the most independent. I did not seem to need her like the others did. I see that as primarily a response to the temperament I was born with, as well as my early decision to develop that protective persona of reducing my needs so I could avoid disappointment. She got the message well."

Fives are conflicted between the need to relate to others and the need to pull back and protect their private holdings, an impulse the Enneagram defines as *avarice*. This is supported by the classical defense of isolation – separating ideas from their original feelings. Enneagram books refer to this as *compartmentalization*, an unconscious mechanism that allows Fives to stay emotionally aloof from highly charged situations. Fives can then minimize the possibility of being overwhelmed by anything they have not already mentally anticipated and maintain a sense of privacy and control while with others.

Just as Fives stay emotionally distant from others who might demand too much, they stay remote from their own emotional truth, often by intellectualizing and rationalizing it away: "I couldn't express my feelings in the couples work with my girlfriend present. I couldn't say anything. In fact, I did not know what my feelings were until I worked with the therapist individually and realized the real reason the relationship couldn't work was because I had no feelings for her. In my head it seemed like it should have been working." A Five's internal emotional isolation mirrors their external reactions to others.

What Brings Fives to Therapy

If Fives overcome their initial reluctance, they are often deeply attracted to psychotherapy as well as the Enneagram. Both provide valuable understanding about interpersonal realms. Both can potentially make Fives even better observers, as well as provide safety in social situations.

Although the detached observer role comes easy to them, Fives often feel lonely and have a genuine desire to have satisfying intimate relationships. D.W. Winnicott's famous statement "it is joy to be hidden but disaster not to be found," speaks to the Five's dilemma in relationships and some Fives start to realize what they lose when they succeed in hiding: "With maturity I realized that something was missing, a void of worth and connectedness. I began to question why I work so hard to just observe. And I began to feel the pain." Another added: "Therapists need to understand that Fives are subtly dissatisfied with their lives. Underneath the intellectual bravado the power of human interaction is missing. They become sour, critical and despairing if they don't change."

What Does Not Work

Five clients can present a blank "poker face" and offer minimal information, unnerving therapists who rely on nonverbal clues to evaluate the progress of therapy. If a Five answers questions slowly an anxious therapist might respond by asking more questions. The Five, in turn, will likely perceive this as intrusive and clam up even more – the beginnings of a difficult transference/counter-transference dynamic.

A different Five client, however, might fill up the room with talk. Some are capable of detailed tangential intellectualizing, something that can distract and confuse the issue at hand. A therapist tempted to match the Five's mental powers could wind up feeling intimidated or inadequate. The therapist would know this has happened when the session feels flat, as though words are flying around the room, at an elevation no lower than the brain. Fives are good at intellectualizing and they can also be competitive.

A Five's social isolation can make them susceptible to exploitation by charismatic therapists or counselors. Ideally, therapy focuses on empowering the client and most therapists are trustworthy. Some Fives, however, reported experiences in which a therapist violated their boundaries. In one case, the therapist consulted with the Five client about his other clients. In another, a spiritual counselor tried to induct the client into a religious cult he was a member of.

Usually when therapy fails with Fives it does so for more subtle reasons. One client described a therapeutic relationship that initially worked, and then later faltered due to unresolved transference and counter-transference. At first, the client found her therapist's warmth and emotional caring helpful: "She seemed to have been a heart-centered type who helped me get more in touch with my heart. Her 'feeling with' empathy was very helpful even though hard to tolerate. I had a sense of being understood, letting up a lot on self-judgment. I do believe I did learn to tolerate intimacy better, and carried that on further in more mutual relationships. It helped me begin to feel safer in revealing myself."

As the therapy continued, however, the client grew dependent on the relationship and consequently more vulnerable. She compensated by acting superior and creating distance: "I began to get angry at her a lot – and it seemed like we reached an impasse. It felt like the classic conflict between the pull of my intimacy subtype into dependency on her, and the reactive withdrawal of my type. I thought, 'you can't need someone that much.' And I think my arrogance was coming in more and more. My sense was the therapist didn't handle it well, didn't understand what was going on, or know what to do about it. She was getting more defensive, which she hadn't before. Then I did the 'totally pulling away and shutting down' trick so I could end therapy on a positive note: 'this has been really helpful, but I feel done.' And she agreed. My sense was that neither of us knew how to get beyond the impasse, so we stopped the therapy. That may have been the best option.

"I do wonder if she had gained a deeper understanding of what was going on with me, if the outcome could have been different. Maybe the therapy really was done. Maybe I was getting angry because I felt dependent and couldn't move on. It's hard to say, except it's so like the issues that come into other intimate relationships – withdrawing when I get too close – that I wonder. Maybe if the therapist had better understood my pulling away, she could have disarmed it."

Recognizing how a Five looks when defended in therapy might have helped this therapist, who could have been caught in feeling devalued by her client. Here is what Fives tell us to look for:

- "I sit rigid, using crossed body language, and give short, intellectual answers. I pass the control over to the therapist. The therapist may think 'this is what it's like to be a Five in therapy' and this would be useful understanding. Use your body to understand me."
- "I can be shut down and become totally unavailable for open-hearted connection. I am highly aware of it but feel unable to do anything about it. In a therapy relationship it plays out to the point where my entire being felt like I didn't want anything to do with this person."
- "I'd be putting on a façade."
- "Remote, removed."
- "I come across as aloof, unaffected and superior."
- "I can get arrogant, come across as the know-it all, ready to shut down the threatening interpretation a therapist has brought out."
- "In therapy Fives may be moving into realms where we feel less confident. Sensing that our intellectualizing is not what's going to get us where we need to go, we may begin to feel we have nothing to offer. This could lead us to cling to what we do feel we have over the

therapist. I may feel vulnerable and like a child, but I'm still smarter than you!"

The Five's defensive strategy is specifically designed to avoid exposure and minimize risk in relationships. So, once Fives recognize a problem, they may still weigh whether going to therapy is worth the price. The process takes time and effort and Fives often want to know what they will get in return for their investment. One Five remembered thinking before therapy: "Do I want to look at my issues? Do I even want to give the time and resources to recognize there is an issue?" In the end, a Five's curiosity about the deeper meaning of life, and the promise of being understood, often wins out.

What Does Work

Most Fives stress that they need to trust a therapist: "It is a risk to step out of being the observer; I need a therapist to tolerate my need for trust." One Five defined a trustworthy therapist as someone who is "clear, knowledgeable, and experienced. Also, knowing what the boundaries are in the relationship helps me avoid social anxiety."

While many Fives admitted that they would probably become defensive if forced into their feelings too quickly, they also warned that keeping therapy on an intellectual level will not create change: "I wish therapists understood that we can be so insightful, but that may not be what we most need. I used to love dazzling therapists with my brilliance. A good therapist needs to see beyond that, while still being suitably impressed! See that all the insight in the world isn't really going to get me where I need to go. If I were to seek a therapist today, I would be concerned that one who is coming from a primarily thinking place isn't going to be ultimately helpful. But the catch-22 is that the therapist who really works towards opening the heart is going to be more threatening. So be aware of that need, and the fear of going there. Go slow."

Fives recommend therapists work with their intellectual defense gently and persistently: "I test my therapists to find out if I can just talk about feelings. I want to know if they can handle it. If they can't/don't, I feel relief along with disappointment and frustration." Therapists need to be able to help Fives access feelings: "I intellectualize so much and am able to control my emotions so well that a predictable therapy situation is not helpful. I am able to assess the experience very quickly and prepare myself for almost anything that might come up (unconsciously), so I need a therapist who understands this function of a Five and knows how to get around it. I need to be drawn into an emotional state rather than a thinking state." Mirroring and empathizing with the Five's emotions are helpful: "Therapists need to be more primitive and give a way to identify and acknowledge my basic feelings. Staying with me intellectually will not help." Another Five added: "I need the therapist to understand how difficult it is for me to be in such a vulnerable situation. It helps if they show compassion, acceptance, warmth and humanity."

Fives also said they need therapists to recognize that their intellectual strengths are an important resource:

- "I need a therapist to understand that knowledge creates power in therapy."

- "It's important to establish the sense that what I may bring intellectually is valuable, especially as I learn to integrate what I know from my heart and my body. That acknowledges what's there, and may make the new territory less scary. It doesn't have to be about leaving the mind behind, or even if we have to do some of that scary stuff, it's about integrating it. The process can establish the sense that we both have something to bring to the table; the therapist is here to help me get more in touch with my heart or gut, and my mind is a valuable tool to bring into the process."

Fives follow a developmental growth arc from ideas to emotions, from acquiring psychological knowledge to integrating their feelings. At different times in their lives, Five clients might look for different capacities in therapists. In an early phase, the intellectual reputation of the therapist could be important. Later, the therapist's relationship skills count most: "In the past I sought therapists who had a particular kind of knowledge, representing the idea of authority about an approach. I had extensive experience with both hypnotherapy and cognitive restructuring. They helped move the knot in my belly around, but never got down to the source of it. Recently I looked for a therapist who was seasoned, had wisdom and maturity, and could offer more of a healing relationship. Now, the knot is softening."

Psychotherapy occurs in a context that is inherently vulnerable. Fives want therapists to understand how much they need to feel safe when learning the unfamiliar language of emotions and interpersonal communication: "In the early phases of therapy, just a little experience of anxiety may be overwhelming. The therapist needs to provide a lot of safety."

Therapists can also inadvertently humiliate Fives by asking them questions they can't competently answer. Questions about emotions, for instance, can be confusing: "It is difficult to answer when asked about feelings, because I don't know how I feel." It may be better to begin with physical feelings: "It is helpful to ask me about my body connections – dry mouth, butterflies in belly. Then I can connect my physical sensations to my emotions."

One Five described a therapist who respected his need for safety by allowing him to retreat into his mind before bringing him back to his feelings: "I tested the therapist by using more humor than the session required. I appreciated how he supported me in the defense for a while and then came back with, 'And what were your feelings when you talked about that issue earlier?' Or 'Let's look at this from another angle.'" The safer the client felt in the relationship the more confident he was about taking emotional risks.

Some Fives say that just being in the reflective atmosphere of therapy awakens their capacity to self-observe and promotes change: "Just understanding that I'm trying not to feel has been helpful. I've been learning to sit back and try to let my defenses fade, so that I can hear the other person. It really helps just to understand what I'm doing and avoiding."

As I mentioned, some Fives are difficult to read and may not talk much, so getting feedback to determine if therapy is on track presents a particular challenge. Fives suggest that we simply ask them if they are comfortable with what is happening. Therapists can ease their own tension and get honest feedback by asking questions like: "Would it be OK for me to tell you what I'm hearing?" Or by soliciting feedback about their performance: "You know, I've been wondering if I'm being helpful, if you're getting what you need." Or a therapist could just ask for more information: "I'm in the dark, tell me more. What is helping, and what is not?" The meta-message in these questions is: "It's important to me to know how you're doing." For Fives, who often feel overlooked, hearing this is good medicine.

Learning the rhythms of the Five processing style also helps. Some Five clients take a long time to answer a question or share a thought; being patient is necessary. Usually, they are focused on replying accurately and authentically: "When I get quiet, this is honest. When the therapist moved in and asked more, while I was still thinking, it started to bring up old memories of being pushed around." It is also important for relational therapists to avoid expecting Fives to show a lot of emotion. A "less is more" approach will leave them room to gradually express their feelings. As one client explained, "What may look to a therapist like a small expression of emotion is a lot for me."

Therapists who interpret carefully will have a good chance of being effective with Fives. Over-interpreting or interpreting too quickly, regardless of accuracy, can feel overwhelming and unsafe to the Five client. One client described a Jungian therapist who "suggested dream interpretations that felt accurate. But, I just wasn't ready for that much truth and the changes I would have to make in my life at the time. So I left therapy." Later, however, the same client found her therapist's interpretations useful: "His interpretations were helpful, even when they were inaccurate, because I could take the information and think about it during the week. This helped me understand myself better. I also got important insights into how others might see me." Effective interpretation also depends on where the authority is placed: "The therapist needs to offer feedback with a take-it-or-leave-it attitude, allowing me a choice."

Relationships are important to Fives and learning more about them is a particular goal of therapy: "When working with the transference and counter-transference, the therapist sharing her observations helped. Afterward I could take away what I learned and think about it. Being truthful and real is helpful. When the therapist gives me honest feedback it can be devastating. But, I will take it and think about it, even if I disagree."

Several Fives added that therapists who sounded judgmental risked losing rapport: "My orientation is to 'what is' and not what 'should be.' If the therapist talks about 'what should be' when I say what is for me, I will stop trying to say what is." It is also sometimes wise to double-check that your Five clients actually hear what you mean to say, as their thinking can take a paranoid direction. If troubling thoughts can be identified and addressed before they harden into conclusions, the therapy will stay on track.

Fives often talk about feeling unseen, both as a source of safety and of sadness. They sometimes act in ways that unconsciously invite being overlooked. In therapy, this might take the form of not offering information unless it is specifically asked for. Being seen and taken seriously by a therapist is one effective treatment for this wound: "I feel recognized when I see my therapist take the time to respond as genuinely and briefly as possible to whatever I say."

Maintaining continuity also helps. If therapists demonstrate that they are paying attention and are aware of issues in an ongoing way, their Five clients will often feel more confident. A therapist could, for instance, begin a new session by saying, 'So, last week we were talking about...'"

Quid Pro Quo

Five clients also mentioned feeling anxious in a therapeutic relationship simply because of its inherent imbalance: "It is so excruciating to be under someone's gaze, being asked to share with nothing given back." Some mentioned needing a sense of exchange, a "quid quo pro:" "I was in therapy for three years before I shared anything significant, I would just deny it if the therapist suggested something might be important, even when it was. I was not comfortable enough to tell her anything until, one day, she loaned me a book off a shelf in her office. I could tell she had read it and was excited about it, and that was a kind of self-disclosure. After that I trusted her."

The safety of therapy can help Fives learn to get more of what they want in relationships. A Five's social self-critic is often severe, and causes them to withdraw because they pressure themselves to perform perfectly even in casual social situations. One Five said that when her therapist owned up to not knowing something she felt reassured. Also: "Hearing first-hand accounts of how others struggle with connecting to their emotions and hearts allowed me to find a few precious threads of commonality."

Discovering that we all say things that aren't quite what we mean and that most people are not severely judgmental can help Fives risk revealing what they think and feel. The Five client's social experiences can also be reviewed in therapy. Client and therapist can brainstorm new possibilities and practice communication. The therapist can also feed back how the Five is probably perceived in social circumstances. The comfort of being accepted by the therapist may ultimately extend to other relationships as the Five becomes more secure.

Many Fives reported that successful therapy helped them lessen their social isolation and reduce the gap between their thoughts and emotions: "It was helpful for me to see the therapist modeling appropriate feelings in response to my experiences, and naming the feeling. Then I could see a story of my life, from the perspective of another, with feelings attached."

When there is sufficient trust in the relationship, the therapist can help the client link current issues to childhood patterns if that is indicated: "Feeling safe and trusting allowed me to be aware of my emotions. I could connect the thought with the feeling and live in it. Then I could look back to an earlier time in my life."

Guided imagery helped some Fives make links between compartmentalized parts of themselves: "With my eyes closed I go into a suspended state where I see a picture from childhood, but don't have the feelings. Therapy helps me attach emotions to it, taking it step by step." If a client unearths a troubling memory and suppressed feelings, the therapist can bear witness, acknowledge the client's feelings and identify any conclusions about life that the child formed. Understanding the impact of the past on the present and making changes are both possible from a ground of emotional safety.

Encouraging a Five to keep a journal of feelings, relationships and dreams can be useful and takes advantage of the Fives' inclination to privately reflect on their experiences. It may also be necessary for the therapist to ask if the client has anything to share in the session. A Five might bring material, but not reveal it unless the therapist asks.

A therapist can also co-opt the Five tendency to anticipate the future – called "previewing" in Enneagram books – by suggesting a theme to work on in a future session. Use caution, though, as Fives can easily perceive suggestions as expectations. You also might ask the client if what she wants from therapy matches your idea of what is important to work on. Encouraging the Five to express their needs and wishes in therapy helps them carry the ability over into their other relationships.

Fives who used meditation as an adjunct resource reported it both beneficial and damaging. One Five who found it helpful said: "I practiced visualizing my chakras opening, especially my heart, like a lotus flower, allowing me to be impacted by others." Another Five had an opposite experience: "The way I practiced meditation alone became a manifestation of my defense, it had to do with visualization, focusing on staying in the light, and I only allowed the good in my consciousness. The pain, grief, sorrow and rage came around to bite me and it was devastating. Group meditation might have helped me stay more grounded." Therapists may want to ask if and how their Five clients use meditation as it can increase their compartmentalization and isolation.

Group Therapy

Some Fives favored group therapy as a way to become more socially comfortable. One Five remembered a youth group that served as an "encounter group light:" "Even though I watched more than I talked, it was a life-changing experience for me. First, I started to see that all these kids that I thought were so different from me were like me. And the extent to which I was able to share myself was profound to me at the time. So depending on where a Five is in their process, they may need the safety of not having to participate too much. That was true for me. In successive group experiences it became easier to share more."

In the early stages of group process it may be difficult for a Five to seek the spotlight and ask to be heard: "My expectation is if I ask for a need to be met my request will be overlooked." One Five felt overpowered because the more aggressive members of his group monopolized all the time and the therapist did not intervene: "Missing the opportunity to break out of my observer role was a loss," he said. Ideally, a therapy group should balance the Five's need to be heard with some sensitivity to their fear of exposure.

Couples and Family Work

Most of us can occasionally relate to George Bernard Shaw's comment, "If only having a social life did not depend on other people," but for Fives it is at the core of life's difficulties. From the perspective of the people near them, Fives often seem to give up without trying and generally need to learn to communicate what they feel and need. They also need to listen to how others feel and respond in turn. Therapists working with Fives in a couple or family context need to appreciate how challenging it is for them, while keeping them engaged in the exchange.

It is also good to explain to other family members that Fives need time to process before they answer a question. Spouses who understand this will be less likely to push for a quick response, and thus avoid causing the Five to further withdraw – a dynamic known to couples therapists as "pursuing-retreating."

Understanding that the Five is working on a response can encourage others to be patient. Asking the Five to let others know when they need time, or are choosing not to engage, is also fair. From the outside, taking time to think and refusing to respond appear identical and Fives may be doing either.

Studying the Enneagram

Many Five clients reported that the Enneagram can be normalizing and helpful, especially for understanding their relationships: "I began to work with a therapist who helped me get more in touch with my heart. I would have conflicts because I could think circles around her and sometimes would get arrogant and feel disrespectful because she didn't understand something at that level. And yet, that wasn't her role – that wasn't what she was bringing to my life. I really didn't need her to be as cerebral as me. But I imagine this could be a common conflict for Fives in therapy.

"Knowing the Enneagram would have helped us understand what was going on in the midst of the situation. I know I have much more appreciation for the heart types in my life now, and they appreciate my insightfulness. We understand that we are bringing each other different gifts. Maybe if I'd understood that before, it would have helped me through my arrogance."

Learning about different personality styles offers Fives a framework for understanding and accepting themselves. It also provides insights that relieve their social anxiety, as well as suggesting a path for further growth.

Connecting Points
Five Connects to Eight

The connecting points of both Eight and Seven offer the Five an expanded sense of self. On the upside of the connection to Eight, the physical and sexual energy generated in this ego-state turns up the Five's life flame and provides raw power for self-direction. Fives are willing to touch and be touched by others when they have an Eight's sense of physicality and abundant confidence.

The connection also brings a difficult, but significant aspect: anger. To many Fives anger is uncomfortable; it feels out of control and frightening. A spontaneous outburst of angry feelings could lead to social mistakes and, subsequently, shame and suffering: "Expressing anger is the biggest taboo for me. This brings me to an interesting aspect of how therapy got difficult; I had a lot of anger coming up towards my therapist and it seemed like neither of us knew how to deal with it. Perhaps working with my anger would have been the key in getting through that impasse. If the therapist had been able to encourage me to express my anger I might have been less afraid of that vital, instinctual energy."

Learning to accept their anger – and to consciously integrate the benefits of instinct and aggression – can be important for Fives. Otherwise they can act out their anger unconsciously in ways they will probably regret. One Five said that just learning about his connection to Eight helped: "Just knowing that anger is part of a person and it's OK to have it, allowed me to work with the fear that I'd destroy everyone. The energy behind the rage was repressing the energy I needed for life. It created a tension that caused depression, even suicidal feelings. The metaphor that helped me is 'Anger is like fire; when you work with fire you can do wonderful things. If you don't work with fire, it destroys.' Fear gets projected into the fire and the anger feels separate from myself, the enemy within. Talking about it helps, but it takes time to trust it."

Five Connects to Seven

Fives caught in the low side of Seven can rationalize being selfish, reframe their behavior to avoid responsibility and magnify their sense of intellectual superiority. They may indulge in monologues about areas of expertise or control conversations with tangential talk. This behavior is often motivated by unconscious fear and can be made use of if the Five learns to notice the behavior and connect it with underlying feelings. For example, one Five observed: "I used to be disarmingly sparkling, witty and entertaining while keeping my emotional reaction to the situation hidden away."

On the high side, the connection to Seven gives Fives more humor, optimism and creativity. They are also more spontaneous and accessible in relationships: "The humor of the Seven's gift of lightness gives me permission to laugh at myself. I can share with others the ironies I see in how I live my life, as opposed to how I want to live. Humor and irony have been wonderful tools for both understanding and owning my rationalizations."

Dreams

Several Fives reported doing dream work in therapy. For some this was helpful, for others it was too intellectual. A number of clients mentioned dreams that represented hot issues for Fives, among them social humiliation and fear of invasion. Flying is a universal dream experience and several Fives mentioned it; one man said it seemed obvious to him that when he flies in his dreams he is observing life from a distance – also his waking tendency.

A common issue for Fives is the double-bind created by clinging to avarice. On the one hand, avaricious Fives avoid the risk of expending their energy. But, they also need things from others. One Five shared a funny dream that alluded to this conflict: "I'm in the back seat of my car at the coffee shop drive-up window. My elderly mother is in the passenger seat and my 10-year-old daughter is driving. I am telling them I want a double mocha cappuccino with skim milk. They keep getting it wrong. Frustrated, I think, "I guess to get what I want, I am going to have to just drive.'"

Good Enough Therapy

Good enough therapy for Fives creates a safe environment that helps these clients experience their feelings. While the Five's intellectual talents are admirable, they are no substitute for relationships, which require access to emotions and are sometimes vulnerable and spontaneous. Acknowledging that others are emotionally important to them, and learning they actually gain more by sharing themselves, are both transformative steps for Fives.

Author Franz Kafka, a likely Five, once said, "you can hold back from the suffering of the world, you have free permission to do so and it is in accordance with your nature, but perhaps this very holding back is the one suffering you could have avoided." Non-attachment – the Five's gift – means being fully involved in your experience and yet being able to let go. Psychotherapy can help by providing a relationship in which the Five can deepen their capacity to be connected to themselves and others.

Sixes

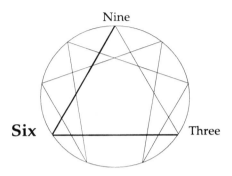

Nine

Six

Three

Presentation in Therapy

• Phobic Sixes may be obviously anxious and scan their environment; some have wide-eyes and staccato speech

• Counter-phobic Sixes may be confrontational and aggressive

• Can offer questioning, "yes-butting," contradictory statements

• May be mistrustful or suspicious of the therapist's authority

• May talk about worst-case scenarios

• Usually perceive themselves as less powerful than others, if not outright victims

• Last minute cancellations are more likely than with other Enneagram styles

• Substance abuse can initially relieve a Six's anxiety and doubt by relaxing the nervous system. When Sixes grow dependent on substances, they can become isolated from others who might provide emotional support and helpful reality checks. Substance toxins can combine with this isolation to amplify paranoia.

At their best, Sixes have an acute mental clarity and are highly perceptive. They have excellent accurate intuitions about situations and people. These abilities lend themselves to skillful problem solving and a creative vision of shared possibilities.

When caught in their unhealthy pattern, Sixes chronically interpret the motivations of others as being malevolent. They can withdraw into paranoia, become accusatory and not follow through on their commitments to themselves or others.

The Six attention style sorts for danger. They are also loyal, possess an offbeat sense of humor and are aware of things that others overlook. Prone to doubt, they can see the other side of any assertion. They question authority, but seek a competent authority to believe in anyway. Sixes manage fear in two, seemingly contradictory, ways: by being phobic and avoiding what scares them or by becoming counter-phobic and challenging their fears. Most Sixes live on a continuum between these two poles.

The prevailing American culture certainly has a fearful streak, but "positive thinking" is part of our idealized image of mental health. Popular psychology also promotes the notions that negative thoughts are unhealthy and being optimistic is ideal. Sixes are well aware of this cultural bias and how their own style differs: "When I imagine the worst thing that can happen and I can accept it, it gives me the courage to proceed. It's actually a good thing." The pressure to think positive directly opposes the Six's core strategy.

Childhood Experiences and Adult Defenses

Sixes have an innate natural faith, based in their intuition, that gives them the courage to meet life in the moment. In childhood, however, they often experience people in authority and positions of trust as unpredictable, deceptive or even dangerous. The degree of this varies, but most Sixes remember feeling that their basic sense of safety and trust was damaged: "My Mom's discipline and behavior were very erratic. My parents frequently fought verbally and physically. I never knew when this would happen, although the tension in the air was often a warning. So I can understand why my fear was ever-present."

Six children learn to avoid surprises by anticipating future harm. While this focus may alert them to actual danger, it also causes them to lose touch with the present and cling to inaccurate fearful assumptions. A Genogram will usually indicate a childhood environment where the Six child's hyper-vigilance and doubting mind were the best defense available.

Sixes guard their world-view with the defense mechanism of projection – attributing to other people or objects, their own unaccept-able thoughts, feelings, motives or desires. When this defense is active, Sixes see their internal issues as belonging to external forces. Projection can be negative or positive, but others are perceived as larger and more powerful. By attributing authority, power or their own unwanted feelings to others, a projecting Six avoids responsibility. This protects a self-image of someone powerless and innocent in the face of conflict or difficulty.

One Six said, "Often I hear the words, 'don't worry' coming out of my mouth to someone else when that isn't really their issue at all. They might be trying to work through a difficult time in their relationship, but they're not saying, 'This is the end of my marriage, I am really worried.' I am. My own reaction is that anxious feeling of impending doom, so I tell *them* not to worry."

What Brings Sixes to Therapy

Sixes are motivated to seek therapy because of chronic anxiety, confusion about relationships and losses. They may also want guidance from a competent authority figure. Also, when Sixes arrive at a calm period of their lives – perhaps they have an interesting, rewarding profession or a stable, loving relationship – their chaotic mental life becomes inconsistent with the facts. They seek therapy to resolve the incongruity and to prevent their anxiety from spoiling a good thing.

If Sixes enter high profile realms – like the business world – without being grounded in solid values, it can precipitate a crisis. They may begin to doubt their competence. Their questioning style and need for group solidarity become liabilities in a competitive atmosphere. They may also feel like victims of their own success: "I wanted to make a lot of money fast. I went into sales and quickly reached the top. But the pressure of what would happen if I wasn't able to sustain my success was overwhelming. I started drinking and felt increasingly isolated. I found help serendipitously."

What Does Not Work

The Sixes I interviewed were unusually prone to perceiving their therapists as failed authority figures. Some felt disappointed by therapists who tried to work beyond their range of competency: "After I was sexually abused by a clergyman, I went to a psychologist and put her on a steep learning curve. I don't think she understood enough about abuse at the beginning. She did not initially advise me to get away from the man or to tell someone what had happened. I was terrified that I would cause the minister harm, and thus stayed silent until I left the church many months later. If the psychologist had explained the nature and outcomes of professional misconduct earlier and referred me to sexual assault services sooner, it would have helped. The therapist did learn and provided useful reports to the church later. But the early days were a problem."

Later, the same Six was referred to a psychiatrist and felt her need for safety was inadvertently overlooked: "I was sent to a psychiatrist for medication when I was suicidal. Once he allowed his receptionist to leave early and I was alone in the building with him. I freaked out, but I could not tell him why until later."

Several Sixes warned against approaches where the therapist's authority or the therapeutic process is unquestioned: "I went to an analytic therapist when I was in a lot of pain. I started this process so I stayed even when it was making me feel worse. I just kept giving my authority away. I stayed too long." Another Six whose therapist's opinions conflicted with his own experience said: "I tried to go with the therapist rather than staying with my own process. When the therapist labeled me, it felt damaging and his interpretations took a long time to undo. Sixes are really good at hiding clues, so he wouldn't have known."

If a therapist responds to a Six's doubt and questioning by trying to pin the Six down, it can make things worse: "In therapy I can be provocative and my insights are contradictory. But, if the therapist can just validate my perceptions, it empowers me. If the therapist needs to spar or argue and therefore assert their authority, then that replicates my problem. But if a therapist is able to be on my side it is the sweetest thing. But I'm thinking why can't I just *let* them on my side? I want it so much, but I'm afraid it will not be sincere or I'll be misused. So I keep my distance and wait."

Some Sixes recalled therapists who were too mental, offering too much information without enough interpersonal connection: "One therapist I had was heady and read a lot. He named things that were happening, but it would set off a long chain of thoughts in my head. He gave me a book to read; it had good ideas, but they didn't help because I needed the ideas to be offered in the context of a relationship."

Other Sixes were frustrated with therapists who did not provide enough context: "I did go to therapists who engaged me cognitively. I went to one who did EMDR. Overnight my nightmares stopped, but I couldn't integrate what happened. I decided not to go back to that person. I wanted to understand the process."

Sixes also say that therapists frequently try to argue them out of their worst-case scenarios: "Worst-case possibilities really do happen to Sixes. It's frustrating when therapists don't believe this." A therapist might try to convince an anxious Six that things are not so bad, a tactic which generally increases the Six's anxiety and sense of alienation. The Six could feel like the therapist doesn't listen well or grasp the complexity of their situation.

Several Sixes mentioned feeling pushed to accept a therapist's solutions. Rather than listening, the therapist might be trying to quell a client's doubts by imposing what the therapist thinks will help. While offering advice can be useful, if the client continually replies with "yes, but", simply repeating the advice may leave them feeling misunderstood.

In transference, Sixes may project their own authority onto a therapist, by either idealizing or devaluing them. A therapist caught in counter-transference with a Six client could become anxious, as if they have subconsciously "caught" the client's nervous hyper-vigilance. The therapist might defend against her own anxiety by playing along with the client's authority projection, acting paternal and reassuring. While this could be temporarily comforting, the client could feel that the therapist has become inauthentic, which would be true and thus confirm the client's sense of distrust.

Some Six clients express their anxiety and doubt by cancelling sessions at the last minute, holding on to the option of therapy while struggling with their ambivalence. Meanwhile, the therapist might experience this as passive-aggressive. The therapist can avoid feeling taken advantage of by addressing any implicit transference and counter-transference as well as by setting clear boundaries.

In the era of managed care – where insurance company representatives, rather than clients and their therapists, decide the amount and types of treatment a client will benefit from – the ultimate authority for treatment may be unclear. For insured Six clients this can be a particular conflict. If the insurance company says a Six client should be finished with treatment after ten sessions and the client is not, who is the authority? Has the client failed if they need more sessions? Since managed care companies are motivated by profit, while clients know their own needs, therapists can use this predicament to explore authority issues and help Sixes get in touch with their own truth.

Sixes say that when they feel defended in therapy they may become phobic and ambivalent, unexpectedly aggressive or intellectual and theoretical:

• "Decision making becomes impossible. I switch from yes to no, back and forth, full of self-doubt and uncertainty. I look to others for answers. I get the urge to run away."

• "I lash out and blame situations or other people for my feelings. I explode with a degree of anger that's out of proportion to the situation. Sometimes I withdraw and become overly emotional, but

cannot identify what is going on. Hence the above problems."
  • "I don't always speak in accessible terms and feeling misunderstood is a huge issue. I get defensive and if my defense is challenged it takes all my constructive energy to protect myself from being misjudged and this prevents the therapy from moving forward. I need the therapist to get around the linguistic impasse, to give me the benefit of the doubt. Don't disagree, or at least be very respectful, nonjudgmental and show an effort to understand."
  • "Give me feedback, but don't fight or engage in conflict or debate."

What Does Work

More than any other Enneagram style, Sixes spoke of the importance of the therapeutic relationship and the therapist's personal integrity. What the therapist did was more important than what he or she said.

Several Sixes recalled therapists who were late for sessions and the anxiety that created. One said her therapist "was late every week. When I finally confronted her she 'owned' the problem. It was important for her to validate me. She said 'I can see how you would be upset.' Most important, she changed the behavior. Her sincerity was critical." Another Six told of a misunderstanding with his therapist over an appointment time where it was unclear who made the mistake. The therapist neither blamed nor apologized but calmly acknowledged the problem and scheduled another time. Another Six said, "My therapist was running late, she apologized but she also provided an example by taking a deep breath and getting present. There are times when she talks a lot. Then she pauses, gets present and just sits with me."

One Six client remembered panicking when her therapist ended each session by asking her if she wanted to make another appointment. The client would spiral into self-doubt, wondering: "Was she trying to tell me I was done with therapy or should be done? Did I have the right to take so much for myself? Did I not deserve another session.... Did she think I was making up problems?"

This was an awakening for me because I sometimes ask clients if they want to schedule another session. While I have a clear idea of what we might work on in the next session, I ask the question to remind the client that it is their choice. It had not occurred to me that the question might stir up self-doubt, although it makes sense within a fearful world-view. These seemingly subtle relationship dynamics demonstrate how the process of therapy often takes place on other levels of the therapeutic encounter, beyond the techniques and inter-ventions that we therapists believe create change.

The Six's search for a trustworthy authority is also evident in how they scrutinize therapists personally: "I can see through fakeness. The therapist has to be real, and if you make a mistake, don't defend it. Validate the issue, have integrity, and apologize." One Six ex-plained: "trust needs to be established new each week. Don't assume because I trusted you last week it is automatic now." Obviously some trust does carry over, but if a Six client has a moment of panic or fear a therapist should not assume too much continuity. It is sometimes important, for instance, to check for skewed interpretations, compar-ing what you just said with how the client interpreted it.

Sixes may attribute omnipotence to therapists and expect them to protect the Six from any possible discomfort. The example of the client who panicked at being alone with her psychiatrist points to several relevant questions about working with this style: To what degree should the therapist anticipate and cater to a Six client's requirements? When does the therapist confront the client's unreal-istic expectations of perfect re-parenting from an infallible authority?

While therapists reading these descriptions could feel they need to be overly cautious with their Six clients, trying to avoid any situation in which a Six might feel anxious is not possible or helpful. In fact, it may be necessary to identify and expose the Six client's demand that others provide them with more safety than is reason-able, since it uncovers a basic dependency that keeps them stuck. They can then take back their projections and claim more of their power. Working directly with this dynamic as it occurs in the therapy relationship can be a golden opportunity for a corrective experience.

The combination of worst-case thinking and projection often leads Sixes to see themselves at the mercy of forces beyond their control. They recommended that therapists initially sympathize with their helpless feelings. The therapist could then ask Sixes what they say to themselves when they feel victimized or have "bad luck": "For me, when things go wrong, I take it very personally and tell myself that it's evidence of what is wrong with me." To help solve an immediate problem, one Six suggested a therapist say: "It sounds like you are being wronged here. Given that, what can you do? What have you done in the past that was helpful when bad things like this happened?"

When working with Six clients who are overwhelmed by fear, one Six recommended that therapists ask: "What would you say to *yourself* in this situation?" The idea is to evoke the client's observing ego and inner authority rather than have the therapist offer advice and opinions. The answer to such a question may also help the Six connect to the real-world events from which a neurotic reaction sprang: "The biggest help is recognizing what is actually going on, even if I don't really understand why I am over-reacting." Another Six asked a prospective therapist to "work to help me realize my own power." Another Six added: "The best therapist would remind me of what I already know, which removes my confusion and distorted thinking."

When a Six client's current reactions remain overwhelming and unchanged by cognitive insights, it pays to search for the influence of past trauma. Some types of guided imagery and unconscious work can clear away a Six's remembered fears and provide a reality check between the present and past. Revisiting past trauma and understanding how the client interpreted these events may also help. The woman who was sexually abused by her clergyman said, "I was especially prone to take on responsibility for the minister's behavior. I also learned that I really believed I was responsible for the childhood problems. When I saw the link between my father and the minister, I understood that I was not responsible for either." Correcting distorted self-blame for the past, empowers a Six to trust what they know in the present.

Another Six added, "A relationship of trust, safety and honesty is essential. I ask a lot of questions. When the therapist answered my questions it helped me to feel safe enough to bring up difficult issues. It was also good to have the therapist 'keep the faith' throughout the therapeutic process. She mirrored faith for me – in myself."

Understanding Fear and Working with Anger

When fearful, Sixes build cases against other people, which sometimes leads to angry outbursts that leave the others feeling blindsided. Then the Six may retreat. This porcupine behavior impacts relationships, causing others to walk on eggshells or just avoid the Six: "What causes the outburst is being unassertive, not expressing the feelings. I have a fear of what will happen if I express a need. The feelings build and this leads to projecting my intent onto others. As a Six I needed to learn to pay attention to these feelings."

"My therapist had me focus on my inner process. He asked me questions like 'When your anger starts, what does it feel like?' I could pinpoint that it began with a tension in my mouth, a tightening in my jaw. Then I could nip the reaction in the bud. Before that, I was emotionally illiterate. I needed to learn what my feelings were, to give them names and understand where they came from." Other Sixes agreed it helps to learn to both identify and communicate their feelings before they intensify: "When working with fear and anger, it helps to see the links before the pressure builds up to high and there is an all out explosion. I've been learning to express something when it's still small, instead of only counting it as anger when it gets big."

Sixes can get suddenly accusatory and angry during the therapy hour, usually in conjoint work. They may then get caught in their own reaction: "After the explosion, I'm aware of the effects of the outburst, the fear of the consequences and negative retribution. My accusing self comes forward and says, 'you have done a bad thing,' 'there you go again.' I feel guilty. It might be difficult to salvage the therapy hour. It takes 15 or 20 minutes for me to recover.

"It is the same as when I was a kid and I tried to get my parents to understand something. I literally saw red, then the objects would fly and I was out of control. Then there really *were* consequences and negative retribution."

Without denying that he needed to change such behavior, the Six suggested that a therapist, "be gentle when confronting the damage. Repeat your observations but be gentle. Allow me to be in denial for a while. I need to hear it, wrestle with it; I may deny it, but I do think about it." The Six also recommended that the therapist stay immediate and specific by asking "'What are you angry about in this moment? What did you just hear? How are you interpreting what was just said?' Or say something like, 'It feels to me like you are really angry right now.' Or ask, 'What are your thoughts at this moment?'"

Sixes tend to see themselves as small and others as big. Immediately disowning the impact of their own aggression protects their self-image as the vulnerable one: "In group work, people have called me on my behavior and taught me to witness my actions. Seeing the evidence contradicts the powerlessness I like to maintain."

Sixes are also loyal and sometimes stay in seemingly abusive relationships, despite feeling angry and resentful. Sixes want therapists to understand that while they may seem loyal to a fault, they are actually looking for security: "You need to understand that loyalty is about survival of the pack. It is about security and looking out for the underdog. When you shift your way of living, you give up relationships that don't fit anymore. Well, you might keep them, but only out of habit. A therapist might therefore ask a question like: 'How is this relationship serving you now?' and begin to explore the deeper meaning of a Six's loyalty."

Projection

In an article in the *Psychotherapy Networker*, Graham Campbell, a specialist in treating anxiety disorders, commented: "Depressed people are sometimes helped by supportive comments. They are like a sponge absorbing what is sent their way. But anxious clients wear a Teflon coating and supportive comments just slide off. Depressed people tend to feel guilty and inadequate. Consequently, they feel they must change. Anxious people also feel guilty and inadequate, but they are more likely to feel that something else has to change. They objectify what depressed people personalize."

Six clients frequently present to therapists as anxious people and moving the locus of control from the external to the internal is crucial for progress. Projection is the Six's "Teflon coating;" it keeps the responsibility on others while the client waits for them or "something else" to change. While this mindset provides a certain psychological comfort – "at least I'm not the problem," one Six said – maintaining it is a self-fulfilling proposition.

To work skillfully with projection, therapists need to understand how it feels to the client: "Basically, what is going on in my head is so much more real than what is actually going on." Many Sixes reported that learning to recognize projections was especially useful to them: "When I was led to see my projections in a gentle way it helped. I am so unconscious to them that to assume that I will always see them is a mistake. Helping me to see the ways that I project, including what I was projecting onto the therapist, was very enlightening."

One cost of projection is that it blocks or interrupts intimacy since Sixes stop seeing others accurately. The truth about others – that they are also vulnerable human beings doing the best they can – is something Sixes accept only when they claim their own power. Sixes advised therapists to help them integrate their power as well as empathize with the vulnerability of others: "It has helped to try to walk in the other person's shoes, to question why would I get so angry about their behavior when I sometimes do the same thing. I needed to accept more responsibility and deal with the complexities of life."

Several Sixes said that learning they had power was important but also difficult because their powerless self-image provides protection: "Situations in which I have more power than others are stressful. I am afraid of success. Therapy helped me to look at my successes and my power. I used to just ignore it when I saw it. I used to give my perspective away immediately. Now I can keep it." Another Six added: "It helps to see other people as having the same insecurities and to see that I have an impact on them. I am powerful and I've avoided admitting it. I've dressed down, driven a beat-up car. If I am prideless and powerless then I avoid envy and vengeance from others."

One Six said his therapist used guided imagery to review his interactions with others during the week, focusing exclusively on the Six's impact on others: "The therapist asked me questions like, 'What did her face look like when you said that?' The hardest defense to give up is seeing myself as more powerless than others. It feels really liberating to give it up, humbling to realize how pervasive it is. Once this realization – that I impact others – started, it really reinforced itself." Seeing that others are equally vulnerable also makes more satisfying relationships possible.

Another outcome of projection is that Sixes can become paralyzed by their fears and overcomplicate courses of action. One useful approach is to help the client break a problem down and make it simple: "Just now, I am barely learning to break things down to manageable pieces. If I am afraid of making a phone call to someone, my therapist will ask me, 'Can you make a commitment to make the call sometime within the next two weeks?' And she will follow up in the next session. Sometimes it helps to have clear directives."

Some Sixes found practical cognitive approaches helpful. They reported that learning about the developmental stages of family life was normalizing and beneficial. Other clients appreciated being offered very basic principles to live by: "One therapist advised me: 'Be useful wherever you can.' I always remember that and it helps me when I'm overwhelmed."

Grounding in the Body

Sixes recommended that therapists help them shift their attention from their heads to their bodies: "I can stay in my mind and intellectualize just about anything. I'm not always aware of my feelings, my heart or my body. My therapist directs me to my heart and places in my body. I resist this and will bounce back into my mind especially when I start to get scared. However, when the therapist gently steers me back towards my body sensations, gut reactions and feelings, it helps." Another Six added, "My early therapy experiences were just about learning to experience my body. This guy just taught me different relaxation techniques. This was 30 years ago and I still use them."

One Six remembered being helped by a hypnotherapist who accepted his doubts, but didn't get caught in them. Instead, he taught the Six to listen to his body: "I saw a guy for five years who wrote a book on hypnotism. He would make up short phrases designed to make me angry and then help me locate my response in the body. I didn't trust him because I don't trust anyone. When I expressed doubt, he would acknowledge it but then encourage me to stay with my body reaction. Something about that has stayed with me."

Several Sixes recommended adjunctive practices like Tai Chi and martial arts for maintaining their connection with their bodies beyond the therapist's office. Massage and other physically relaxing experiences also helped. One Six, a victim of sexual abuse, said that "Model Mugging," a self-defense training program, was "incredibly helpful" for decreasing her fear and increasing her confidence.

Model Mugging retrains the body memory and mind-set of the victim so she can react differently when anticipating or remembering an assault. This is done by physically reenacting attack scenes in a supportive group setting, with well-padded instructors playing the assailant. The aim is to teach the participant to set strong boundaries and fight back effectively.

An assault victim with any Enneagram style might benefit from this type of work. However, for the Six above, who knew the Enneagram and found the unhealthy aspects of her Enneagram style amplified by her assault, Model Mugging profoundly lessened her fear and self-doubt.

Therapists who offer Six clients a calm, grounded attitude and occasional silence can help: "I have a big circle of people and ideas I run around in, and I need grounding. The best therapist for me is someone who is integrated in heart, head and body and who approaches me from a deep spiritual place. The therapist reminds me to slow down and be in my own body and learn to let messes be. I also need help with re-experiencing memories and tying feeling states to them. It's comforting if a therapist can just be with me when there are no answers. Sometimes there aren't words and just being silent helps me access my integrated core self."

For Sixes, letting go of their mental defenses long enough to experience their feelings requires courage. Therapists can guide them through this unfamiliar territory: "Once I began doing serious, deeper work, the lessons had to be experiential. As is often said, 'the only way out is through' and it feels especially true for Sixes. The need to include bodywork and a heart connection is huge.

"My greatest fear was losing my mental sharpness. I had visions of turning 'California.' In the end, I did lose some of my mental sharpness but I gained a heart. I wouldn't go back for anything. Also, I had to find my way to faith. The absence of trust applied to all my relationships including spiritual ones. Once I made that leap, I found my own authority." Another Six added: "Gestalt therapy, in particular, was especially useful for getting me out of my head."

It also helps for therapists to encourage Sixes to be honest about what they want, and to work with any fears that this admission may produce. The therapist can guide the Six to attend to body clues while visually imagining various scenarios and their outcomes; including what it might be like if the Six went after and got what he or she wants.

Retelling Stories

A technique called "retelling a story," developed by linguist Michael White, is especially useful with Sixes who have unjustified self-blame and doubt. This approach, part of *Narrative Therapy*, says that the reality we live is based on the stories we tell ourselves and, by changing our stories, we can change our reality. A Narrative therapist generally encourages clients to examine their history for personal strengths. The client is helped to gather information that contradicts their "problem-self" story and to then re-tell their story in a way that empowers them. This can be especially helpful for trauma survivors who tend to blame themselves and are often unjustly blamed by others as well. People in the client's community are selectively employed to help re-write the client's story. The therapist plays the role of advocate-coach.

One Six recounted her experience of this technique at length: "My sexual abuse counselor explained that Narrative is based on the idea that we all have many different stories that we can tell about our lives. The therapy helped me reframe my life stories and let go of stories that I saw through the eyes of my perpetrators. The story of my early abuse was based on the belief that I was responsible for what my perpetrators did to me. This I did not realize until I was abused by the church minister, and began to live out that story in relation to him also. My sexual abuse counselor helped me to see how my earlier stories had led to me applying that view to my recent abuse and had been severely damaging to my view of myself. I have also been unaware as to how pervasively my childhood abuse had affected every aspect of my life. My Narrative counselor encouraged me to look at my life and contact those people who I knew had a different view of me. In particular, with regard to the current problem of recovery from clergy abuse, I was able to contact old friends outside the church and get their view of the situation. I was amazed to hear their positive view of myself and their disbelief of the minister's story about me. One particular male friend of my husband said 'I cannot believe that the Jackie I know would set out to 'seduce' anyone.' This helped me to reframe my own view of myself and my life.

"It was also interesting that my friends outside the church were most concerned about the minister's behavior towards me whereas people inside the church commented on my perceived behavior. Consequently, I have been able to look at my history more positively, to see the little girl I was and get more in touch with her goodness, to see the damage to my life which the perpetrators have caused and to get in touch with those who are supportive of me. In the bad times, I try to remember the way my counselor approached my stories and to reframe my thoughts."

Narrative Therapy can help Sixes offset their tendency to re-frame negatively by learning to positively reframe in a Seven-like way. If the Six has been injured by an authority, the therapist can evoke this style's capacity to question authority and put it to good use; helping the Six identify how much they were damaged or treated unjustly. Re-telling their story puts new power in a Six's hands, helping them to further develop their inner authority.

Connecting Points
Six Connects to Nine

The connecting points of both Nine and Three help Sixes become grounded in their feelings and realistically oriented to the external world.

A healthy connection to Nine helps Sixes enter and stay in their bodies; they sometimes report this as a relaxed body feeling most easily found on vacation. Several of the vignettes in this chapter illustrate the healing benefits of this connection; it helps Sixes contact emotions like sadness and love more readily. This also helps them appreciate the best intentions of others. When Sixes have a strong body sense they can distinguish between intuition and paranoia more effectively.

On the down side, Sixes in a Nine ego-state often avoid offering their opinions or taking stands that could lead to conflict with others. They may be unconscious to what they really want and focused on scrutinizing or placating others. Doing this costs them, but they may blame that on authority figures, outside circumstances or bad luck. Getting caught in inessential details while procrastinating is also a negative aspect of this connection. Sixes can also take a Nine-like passive-aggressive approach to conflict.

Six Connects to Three

A healthy connection to Three helps Sixes pursue what they want and brings an optimistic confidence that helps them achieve their goals. Fulfilling their heart's desires can also get them in touch with their emotions.

On the low side, their connection to Three can lead Sixes to overwork and exhaust themselves. They can also be disingenuous and attached to image. Some Sixes are competitive, often in ways that leave others feeling surprised and blindsided: "I find ways to compete. Mentally I'm looking for an angle I'm entitled to. I pretend to not be competing, but I'm really competing on the side." Like Ones, Sixes may also secretly want what they disdain in others.

Dreams

The following dream was reported by a Six woman trying to decide whether or not to quit her job. The dream's intensity and the humor are markers of the inner life of Sixes: "Several years ago I was debating (and debating and debating) about whether or not to leave my corporate job. Though clearly the job was making me crazy and I needed a break, it was too scary to just walk away and suddenly be jobless. I kept waiting for them to offer a golden parachute so I could walk away with money in my pocket, a little cushion to land on. To me it felt like jumping off a cliff, though I had a friend who said, 'take a good look at that cliff – it's about one foot high.'

"During this time I had a dream populated with people in my office. We were all working on a project that had a deadline (as usual in real life). I was running around trying to attend to the details (as usual in real life) and feeling very nervous. I was looking for a certain person to get some information from, and I was told he was in this one certain area. When I got there, a line had formed, and I automatically got in line. It was moving slowly and when I got a little closer I realized that there was a gallows and everyone was standing in line waiting to be hanged. I quit the job."

Good Enough Therapy

It takes courage for Sixes to live in the present when their minds are busy warning them about future disasters. Therapy can provide a safe place where Sixes can explore their desires and realistically assess their fears. Their childhood wounds about authority need to be validated and understood. A Six client may want a therapist to listen to their negative fantasies about the future. But, ultimately, the therapist will need to help their client open up to the full range of possibilities, including what the Six most desires.

Sixes also need to be helped to recognize their impact on others. As they become more grounded in their bodies and emotions, they are better able to distinguish between their intuitions and their projections. By being a trustworthy, appropriately competent "authority figure," the therapist can offer the Six client a model for how to reclaim their own authority and truly individuate.

Sevens

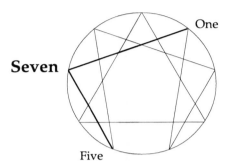

Seven

One

Five

Presentation in Therapy

- Seven clients can appear curious and interested, often minimizing their actual pain and difficulty
- They may be charming and self-referencing; can positively spin their role in a problem
- They can project an air of superiority about how to live
- May use excessive, exaggerated positive words like *fabulous, fantastic, wonderful, the greatest*
- Many Sevens initially come to therapy as part of a couple or family; can mentally understand their problem and then "flee into health" to avoid real change
- They occasionally seek individual therapy to change painful relationship patterns or resolve childhood trauma
- Can be critical and confrontational if they feel limited or pinned down by a line of questioning
- Substance abuse may develop if the Seven's need for unlimited positive options is frustrated by pain and difficulty. Sevens can be aggressive when rationalizing their addictions – reframing other people's concern as their problem. Becoming sober and feeling the pain they have been medicating sometimes precedes psychotherapy.

Healthy Sevens have a joyful, enthusiastic sense about life, are attracted to beauty and have an expansive sense of possibility. They value other people and are unusually accepting and tolerant.

When caught in their unhealthy pattern, Sevens are self-doubting, anxious and manage their fears by obsessively focusing on their own interests and plans for future pleasures. They see others as narcissistic extensions of themselves, either as companions or audiences. If others limit the Sevens they become a source of irritation.

The Seven attention style fixes on positive futures. They have a quick mental energy that helps them connect ideas and see the big picture. They easily engage others with their active, charming, entertaining relational style. American culture amplifies the persona of the Seven with messages about staying young, having fun, and denying limits. The idea that shopping is patriotic, for instance, rationalizes addiction and encourages people to medicate their pain.

Childhood Experiences and Adult Defenses

Sevens have an inherently joyful nature and live in the moment, whether pleasant or unpleasant. As children, however, they become afraid that they can't depend on others to give them the attention they need. Seven children learn early to compensate for any environmental limits by using their abundant creativity to imagine adventures and concoct a happy way to see life.

They also learn to disconnect from pain: "When I was a kid, my dad worked for a major oil company and we were transferred every few years. I make friends easily, but I always had one VERY BEST friend. We would grow very close and then I would have to move away. It was terrible. But, my mom (another Seven) was always quick to point out that I'd make new friends in the next town. She encouraged me to plan ahead and look forward to the future.

"I remember one afternoon, in particular: My mom was overjoyed because she had just found out we were being transferred from a small Oklahoma town to New Orleans. I LOVED our rural neighborhood. We had named all the hills and ponds and had so much fun catching horned toads and riding bikes. But Mom had us holding hands with her and dancing in a circle singing, 'We're moving to New Orleans!' All I felt was fear and misery.

"After a few moves, I think another tendency kicked in, too. Once I knew the transfer was imminent, I began to disconnect from my very best friend and from that town in order to avoid the pain when the disconnection hit full force.

"I still do this sometimes today. When I feel a relationship is ending, I begin to disconnect in advance of the actual ending. This helps me avoid pain. I look ahead to what relationship will be next and imagine how nice it will be."

This habit of keeping lots of future pleasures in mind is an expression of what Enneagram books call "gluttony," a way that Sevens escape their pain through mental and physical appetite: "I am aware that at an early age I had an increased sensitivity that my needs were not being met by others, so I decided to meet them myself. In order to avoid pain, I have to keep my attention and energy on options, or pleasant possibilities." Sevens often remember being the family "fun leader," in charge of keeping others "up and happy." They may later replicate this role in adult life.

When they talk about their childhood and family experience, Sevens often minimize the impact that authority had on them. They can also reframe difficult memories as positive: "Sure, my parents fought a little and drank some, but it's what helped me become independent and successful." Sevens are fearful people who don't sound fearful.

A Seven's preoccupation with unlimited options is protected by the defense mechanism of *rationalization,* which allows Sevens to ascribe acceptable or worthwhile motives to thoughts, feelings, or behavior which really have other unrecognized motives. To rationalize is to unconsciously justify: "My first marriage was 'open.' All the good reasons for this seemed obvious. I told myself this openness is the only way to live. By drinking from this cup of wine for this interest and that cup to satisfy another desire, it felt like there were no limits.

"This rationalization worked until I realized the futility of it; my husband became too attached to the other woman, who was my best friend, and I was in love with two men. I couldn't have what I wanted with either of them. I was afraid of being alone. I realized the greater adventure is to really experience the depth of one relationship and that meant commitment."

What Brings Sevens to Therapy

Sevens who initially come to therapy for relationship work sometimes stay on individually, although the therapist may have to convince the Seven that she is competent and that therapy can make life better. "I present with an attitude of: 'I'm here but I don't have any problems.'"

Sevens often present therapists with an attitude of detached curiosity, even when conditions are severe: "I was totally unable to get grounded. I was having panic and anxiety attacks. I was married to an alcoholic and scared. I took a class taught by a therapist who practiced T.A. It was interesting; I went on to try some individual sessions." Another Seven adds: "I went to therapy because I was in graduate school for counseling and wanted to learn about therapy. Interesting: now as I think about it, my marriage was falling apart and I was in pain."

Sevens can also enter therapy to *avoid* pain: "I went in because I was in pain about a relationship, hoping the therapy could help me feel better." Even suicidal impulses could stem from the same motivation: "When I experienced real depression, like more than an hour, I didn't want to get up, get dressed – nothing mattered for three months. I had suicidal thoughts, but as a way to avoid pain. If a Seven commits suicide it would probably be spontaneous."

Some Sevens have to become deeply uncomfortable in order to penetrate their own denial: "It was the worst month of my life. My daughter was a student at Columbine High School on the day of the famous shooting. My relationship ended, my finances were a mess, my best friend almost committed suicide, and there was no escape. I started having panic attacks and I finally started to admit how bad things were. I made appointments with several therapists to get their support and perspective." Several Sevens reported that they began therapy by making appointments with several different therapists, something I have not noticed other personality styles do.

For Sevens, therapy is a place to express parts of themselves that don't fit their sunny image:

• "We are so good at cheering others up so when we go to others to be cheered up they let us down."

• "It's my job to be 'up.' You don't want to burden your friends with it when you aren't up. There is a lot of pressure to be happy. So I went to a therapist to talk about the down side."

What Does Not Work

Sevens offered numerous stories about how therapy failed them. Some reported that their defenses effectively kept therapists from seeing their underlying pain and difficulties. Sevens can export their belief that others unnecessarily dwell on the negative. Wanting only good news, they can be angry and shocked at unpleasant feedback. Being confronted may feel to a Seven like being trapped and they can be quick to "shoot the messenger." Significant others and even therapists may unconsciously avoid displeasing Sevens by offering them only positive feedback, which the Seven accepts only too easily.

When Sevens feel therapists don't understand their real issues they can adopt a stance of mental superiority: "I wish psychotherapists would understand, my mind is working faster than theirs." This attitude can be off-putting to the therapist, who may then distance the client. Many reported failures seemed related to such transference/counter-transference dynamics.

If a therapist starts feeling entertained by a Seven client's charming personality, it is wise to be suspicious: "I used to go to marriage therapy and charm the therapist. Then I thought, 'This is stupid, I'm paying for this and lying.' I also thought they should be smarter. I'd given them too much credit and I was disgusted. It was a game."

Several Sevens described therapeutic approaches that matched their habitual mental defenses. While helpful with some symptom resolution, these treatments steered clear of underlying feelings and more substantive change:

• "In couples work, the therapist used reframing to help me see the positive intention in my boyfriend's behavior. This helped me see how I was responsible too, and there were things that I could change, which was a good thing.

"However, reframing and learning to apply the Enneagram all increased my chances of creating a positive interpretation. It was all mental, and I was able to breeze right through. The therapy just helped me stay in the relationship too long. I needed to break out of my head strategies and positive reframing to know what I really felt."

• "We did couples work and individual work with a therapist using NLP. It helped with some symptoms I was having, but stayed on the surface, not dealing with any feelings. We were both heavily into substance abuse, she was alcoholic and I was co-dependant and we were both smoking pot all the time. He never asked those questions."

• "I needed a systemic approach to get the big picture, a purely psychodynamic approach did not work, insight alone was not enough to enhance change."

On the other hand, it can be counterproductive for therapists to pursue their Seven client's feelings too aggressively: "I went to a group through the counseling center in college. I could see their deal was to strip away my defenses. I said to myself, 'I've spent 23 years building them, I'm not giving them up now.' I was out of there." This person may have been referring to a "T-group," which was a briefly popular trend in the 1960s, and emphasized an atmosphere of group trust. Sevens want therapists to remember: "Fear and pain feel like they will never end if I allow myself to feel them."

Any approach perceived as authoritarian, absolute or too directive is also guaranteed to fail: "One therapist's behavioral approach did not work for me. It just felt like being told what to do."Another Seven client told this story: "The first time I went to therapy it was because my wife wanted me to. The therapist asked why I was there and said 'if you are going to come here you have to have goals.' Then he offered his hypothesis that I was mad at my father. Looking back on it, I probably was, but I wasn't going there, especially with that therapist. Then he started coaching me about how he wanted me to express this anger. I never went back."

Therapists can better succeed with Sevens if they understand how these clients appear when defensive:
  • "I think psychotherapists and counselors need to understand that when a Seven says everything is great, it may be the view the Seven wishes to believe rather than the way he or she truly feels. Because the Seven likely has no idea how he or she feels. As a Seven, I need help in getting in touch with my own feelings."
  • "Having an idealized self-image feeds my conflict avoidance. I just want to stay in the big picture." Sevens say they need their therapists to allow them to feel adequate control, but still name and define what needs to change.

The therapist confronting the Seven's defense needs to avoid making them feel trapped, which can instigate a counter productive reaction: "I always resist whatever drags me down into the mundane world." Another Seven warned: "When my charm fails, I may get angry about being 'misunderstood.' If you are challenging my positive self-image you are clearly misunderstanding me."

Like Twos, Sevens frequently mentioned dual relationships with their therapists. They often idealized the therapist and sometimes the therapist breached treatment boundaries, perhaps in response. One Seven client wound up editing her therapist's book; another joined a book club with his therapist. Several Sevens explained how and why this happens:
  • "With therapists, I always try to draw little lines around what we have in common. This makes us equal, and then I feel safer."
  • "I am trying to be liked, I want friends, lots of friends. I can't trust you like me if you are not my friend."
  • "Sevens are fearful of authority. So friends are safer than therapists."

Most of the Sevens spoke of the blurred boundaries with little concern, although they were not planning to return to the friend-therapist for further treatment either. Although the Seven client needs their defense respected, good therapeutic boundaries are still crucial: "I tried to make friends with my therapist and she provided wonderful boundaries. If I could have made her my friend she would have been of no great value to me. But, it helped for her to be friendly and to know she would have liked to be my friend."

What Does Work

When the conditions are right, it can be easy to get past a Seven's defense: "I went into therapy guarded intellectually, looking upbeat and cheerful, seeing the sunny side of life. I told myself, 'I'm here, but I don't really need to be here.' It was helpful that the therapist challenged this attitude right away by saying, 'you don't have to be in therapy unless you want to.'" Sevens also have this advice for therapists: "The predominate thing is to recognize when we are masking, to keep us in the truth and give us information. It soothes our anxiety and acknowledges the strength of our mental functioning."

Reframing

Sevens use *reframing* to avoid difficulty as well as to face it. One Seven said: "I want a therapist who treats me like an equal and is authentic. Someone who has had a lot of experience and can reframe anything painful that I discover." Several Seven clients had suggestions about how to handle defensive reframing: "Reframe back. Tell us, 'There is a lot you are missing out on, think of all the interesting experiences lost to you when you avoid your own depths." Or remind them that: "Other people go into their negative feelings and find great value." They also recommended that therapists help Seven clients notice any patterns in their history that have led to accumulated losses: "Take an inventory of a Seven's relationship history. Ask them 'What losses have resulted from your narrow focus on the positive?'"

Sevens say that when a session becomes emotionally difficult, their commitment to stay present may flag. They might also start to rationalize or argue against the value of staying with the difficult material: "I do tend to dismiss serious stuff, to see the glass as half full and this keeps me from seeing my pain." A Seven client could tell a story that positively reframes their role in a problem or even reframe their reframing: "Reframing is both a curse and a blessing, it is a form of denial, but also a form of revelation. I can see things in many different ways."

Sevens recommended that therapists help them recognize when and what they are avoiding. One Seven suggested a "confusion" technique to counter his charm and rationalizing: "Point out the discrepancies in what I'm saying. Say something like, 'I'm confused, you said this, but you also said this, can you help me understand?'" Another Seven said: "Confront my spin and hold steady. You might also start to ask about my immediate motivation and feelings."

Other Sevens suggest exploring why having flexibility and choices is so important to them. Therapy can provide an opportunity to edge near their fear of being limited. The therapist could ask questions like, "What will happen if you are limited? What does this feel like? Have you felt this before?" Deeper issues and grief may come up.

It is also helpful to emphasize equality and teamwork in the treatment relationship:

• "Frame the relationship to me as 'we are working together.'"

• "Treat it like a game we are playing together, like solving a mystery or puzzle."

Deconstructing Charm

Being in therapy causes anxiety and it is useful to remember that Seven is a fear type, since they mask their fear with charm. Sevens offered the following to help therapists understand and defuse their resistance:

• "Charm is always my first defense, the therapist needs to call me on it without embarrassing me. A good thing to say might be, 'Do you need to come up for air? Do you need to take a breather?'"

• "Point out there is a choice of directions to go in when a diversion is brought up. Which direction leads away from pain? Which direction leads towards pain? Underscore that it is a choice. If they choose to go toward their pain, ask them what it would be like to stay there?"

A woman remembered a therapist who used Transactional Analysis: "When I was using the charm defense, the therapist would say: 'you have such a wonderful little kid inside of you.' She would acknowledge my defense without criticizing and then gently lead me back into my sadder feelings. I needed her to recognize both the happy kid and the sad feelings, to allow me to have both. I have a huge inner critic. After I felt safe enough with her, she could become a 'good' parent. The therapist needs to acknowledge all the pieces of the Seven so they can learn to accept themselves."

Understanding How Fear Drives Thinking

Sevens can look like they know what they want, but fear and anxiety may drive this appearance:

- "A Seven can look like they are moving quickly when it's all mental. I always want to look like I'm handling it."
- "There is an argument between my head and my heart."

Sevens mentioned a variety of therapeutic methods that helped them get past anxiety and listen to what they really wanted:

- "I was too afraid to stay where I am long enough to know what I want. I needed to learn even to go to a restaurant and sit with myself and wait until I really knew what I wanted. It helps to be reminded to check with each internal part. Voice dialogue with energy work helped me to get to know the different parts of my self, not just my head."

Some Sevens suggested that therapists listen and initially accept their ideas without interpretation, but also give them suggestions and metaphors to process later:

- "When people come up with something too quick, I can't absorb it right away. If it's critical, my first response to an interpretation or suggestion is usually 'no.' My best therapist gave me metaphors; the images stayed with me and I could unpack them later."
- "Don't discount my thoughts. I need to say and hear them and sometimes they stir up emotions. But, my emotions speak in a little voice."

Therapists also need to understand that a Seven's underlying fear can come out as anger: "If a therapist makes emotional demands on me, I may lash out with anger and criticism. It's good then if the therapist can probe for what I'm afraid of." Another Seven added: "When what I've said is fed back to me, it helps, but it may make me angry. It makes me feel like there is a limit, but I also really need that."

Sevens also suggest that the therapist help them see the positive in what seems negative: "Speak to the part of me that needs and wants to grow. Say something like 'This is your chance to be heard, to get to know parts of yourself that are unique and valuable.'" It is important for the Seven client to know that facing difficulty and pain is their choice – and that it's survivable.

Working with Emotions

When working in depth, a Seven's emotional states can change quickly as they shift in and out of their pain. As one Seven explained: "The thing the Seven fears the most is emotion. In the beginning the Seven won't go anywhere besides their head. The Seven has no idea about their emotions. The therapist has to help them negotiate this terrain. I shift in and out of pain fast." Another Seven added, "If things get too intense, I have to come up for air."

When a Seven client comes out of pain too fast, Sevens suggest that the therapist ask questions like: "That was quick, what got you to recover so fast?" or "Are you sure you're not covering your pain?" or "Do you think you're just not sad?" As one Seven explained: "I'm naturally buoyant. When I decide to lift up out of a painful state, I have a wide array of tools to boost myself up." Sevens also suggest that therapists double-check whether cheering themselves up is really serving them or whether they think they need to stay with their pain a little longer.

Sevens sometimes believe they need to stay "up" for their therapist's sake: "When we pop back from pain too happy and too fast we may be picking up on the cue 'you want us to feel better, so we have to feel better.'" "I also might be taking care of you by being happy. We expect ourselves to be happy and we believe everyone else expects us to be happy too." These mood shifts are usually automatic. The therapist giving feedback can help the client be aware of the behavior and understand their motivation.

Most Sevens said it was important to get in touch with their bodies, especially when their minds are over-active: "I allowed myself to check in with my own feelings and to trust those feelings as valid and important signals about life. Instead of letting my head decide what life was about, I started listening to my heart and my feelings. If it didn't feel right, I no longer talked myself into thinking it was okay, I could finally experience an entire spectrum of reality. I appreciated being encouraged in therapy to stay with the feelings, even if they were uncomfortable. Stay with them and see them through to the other side. I had always cut off all of my uncomfortable feelings before, and so I had never reached the other side."

Sevens tend to be distracted by visual stimulation, which can keep them up in their minds: "Closing my eyes cuts out distractions. My therapist used visualization to connect my body experience with my emotions." To keep them on-track they recommend that therapists: "Ask direct questions and help me connect with my body."

Being present as well as patient may be necessary: "Active listening helps. It's important for the therapist to not move into problem solving too quickly." And the therapist needs to let the Seven client know there is meaning and value in staying with feelings: "The worst thing about suffering is to believe I wouldn't get some kind of gem out of it. If I believe I will, it makes the suffering bearable."

Other ways therapists helped Sevens deepen their feelings included:

- "Assignments to paint my feelings and draw painful elements of childhood got me out of my head and into feelings – got me out of 'fantasy land' and into 'action land.'"
- "Hypnosis got to my feelings and grief as well as a bigger picture of myself."
- "Use humor, with direct and gentle answers."

Some Sevens sounded like Fours when they spoke about the value they found in staying with their pain and their grief:

- "As I surrendered to my grief, the polarity offered a soothing peace."
- "Getting to the full range of feelings is the most honest and clear place you can be, I can relate to Fours, I don't want someone to change the song on the radio that makes me feel sad about what I'm working with, I want to stay with the feeling."
- "In the process of deconstructing my ego – who I've taken myself to be – I've realized that deep feelings are on the same wavelength as sobriety."

Learning Boundaries and Self-Protection

When Sevens optimistically anticipate the future and remember only the positive, they can forget to realistically protect themselves in the present. One Seven found that, "journaling helped me recognize when I reframe and rationalize to forget pain that has occurred over time. For example, I was going to visit my father and stepmother whom I hadn't seen in a long time. It helped me to reread my old journals because they forced me to remember how difficult the relationships were. I don't want to anticipate negative experiences. But, there it is in detail and I am able to protect myself."

Sevens appreciated therapists teaching them about boundaries and self-protection. They can enter situations naively, even when the likely outcome is injury. They needed their therapists to help them moderate their positive thinking and recognize negative possibilities:

- "For the therapist to watch my husband say, 'I don't have time for you,' forced me to hear it without reframing. It became more real to me when someone else heard it."
- "I tend to trust a lot right away; I'm too optimistic. Like I believe that everyone is a good person and they aren't going to hurt me. When that isn't true I become disappointed big time and close the door. My therapist has helped me learn to stay in reality."
- "Counselors need to understand the black/white thinking of a

Seven. If, for example they encourage a Seven to drop away her self-protection and enter life, they need to help the Seven keep the healthy parts of self-protection. Life may not be all bad, but it certainly is not all good, and they should not make themselves vulnerable to attack."

Some Sevens see their anger in relation to boundaries:

• "Because I am dissociated from my feelings I go a long way before I know I'm resentful or angry. That anger is actually a correction and a lead into where I need to be."

• "It would be helpful to present anger as new territory to be explored. Learning to notice feelings and get more into my gut energy helps me to know sooner and speak up about what I am feeling."

Developing Empathy

Sevens do not want others to limit them, yet they often limit others when they resist facing difficulties. One Seven said, "I lose patience when others (spouse) stay in their misery and don't hear my side. When something goes wrong I want to fix it and make it better right away." Another Seven added, "I made light of other people's worries because I didn't want to dwell on the negative. And I shut myself away from my own feelings because they might not fit with the way I wanted life to be.

"Now I am giving myself permission to feel bad sometimes. I can go there without having to fix it and make it all happy right away. I can also hear worries and fears expressed by other people without feeling that I have to make them feel better. I am more alert to my feelings of discomfort, and I am listening to these important signals."

For the fearful Seven, who is intolerant of their own difficult emotions, staying with another person's difficulty can be equally challenging. Learning to feel compassion for others can be an important therapeutic gain. One therapist used guided imagery to help her Seven client empathize: "I was having trouble with my Eight daughter. The therapist had me close my eyes and led me through what it is like to be an Eight. This allowed me to approach her with more compassion and understanding."

Conjoint Sessions

As mentioned, Sevens can easily overreact to being confronted with a problem. It can be difficult for them to hear that others disagree with them or don't see them in a positive light. Their image of being easygoing hits a defensive edge fast and they can become rigid with fear and anger. I have seen Sevens in couples work who seemed to be Ones or Eights until I saw them again outside of the conflict. One

Seven said: "It is terrifying to be criticized; if you are criticized you won't survive because your sense of self is so fragile. If you don't agree with my idea, it feels like you don't like me. I had to learn boundaries, particularly between ideas and feelings."

When Sevens resist facing problems in relationships, their friends and intimates may experience them as superficial and narcissistic. Carried to an extreme, this tactic can result in the loss of important relationships, potentially a major blow to the Seven's idealized self-image. It is during this life passage that we often first meet Sevens in therapy. One Seven said when his wife left him he saw how his rationalizing and refusal to allow feelings caused him this loss. He decided to confront his persona and change: "My charm and ability to get people on my terms just led me to the fire. When things fell apart, I decided 'this is not just a divorce from a woman, this is a divorce from an identity.'"

The Seven's fear of abandonment is stirred up by conflict. They need to see that being present with conflict will have some benefit, even if they have to experience pain. Examining what is really being said and what is being heard is helpful. This provides an opportunity to check out fears before they are foregone conclusions. Therapists might also appeal to the Seven's sense of fairness when they are refusing to listen to another's point of view. When working with Sevens it is helpful to point out their vulnerability to criticism. Giving them feedback about one area of their behavior does not mean they are unappreciated in other ways. As one Seven said: "Break it down. Tell me the parameters of the criticism. Then I can look at it." Supporting Sevens when they are courageous enough to stay with difficulty helps: "Encouragement and compliments are right on the money."

When a Seven's self-idealizing is causing conflict in relationships, I have found a technique created by Jerome Wagner to be useful. Both members of a couple are encouraged to list their consciously embraced qualities, calling them "me." Each then lists their dispossessed or "shadow" features, which are called "not me." For example, if a Seven identifies with being optimistic, they automatically write "pessimistic" in the "not me" list. After the lists are complete, a brainstorming session follows. The topic is: Are there any hidden benefits that the "not me" qualities might have? For example, how might an eternal optimist benefit from sometimes being pessimistic?

This exercise takes advantage of the Seven's ability to see the big picture and make creative connections. It encourages both members of the couple to see their shadows – what they have projected onto each other – and shift their focus to working on themselves.

Family of Origin Work

Sevens sometimes replicate their early role of cheerleader and try to keep people happy in their present life. Playing this role sometimes becomes a burden, which the Seven resents. Sevens can feel and sound martyr-like when they are describing their relationships: "I'm always expected to take care of everyone, or entertain you all and make everyone happy."

When Sevens do family of origin work, negative feelings may surface about this early role they had to play. One Seven said that therapeutic letters – those you write to express your feelings, but do not send – were especially helpful at this stage of his therapy.

Reconstructing the past provides Sevens with an opportunity to explore what they have avoided; what the past was really like versus how they imagined it and how they repeat the past in the present. When the Seven understands the role they have played in relationships through this lens it can be a revelation: "When we went to a Bowenian systems therapist, I saw patterns showing up and got the big picture for the first time. The problems were not just all about her."

Groups

When Sevens have enough trust in a therapeutic group, receiving feedback can be especially powerful: "One day I went to group depressed. I asked them to get me out of it, they said 'no, we think you need to stay there,' convincing me I should stay with sadness! I asked: Because it's good? They said no. Because it's a jewel? Each spin was met with 'no, you should stay with the pain anyway.' I did, and it changed me." Another Seven said: "I was in a group, we did a self-inventory followed by feedback given in a direct way. It was painful to have my self-image challenged, but good for me to look at."

Another psycho-educational therapy group offered the same Seven peer support and normalizing information during a time of loss: "When I went through my divorce all the losses were devastating. The pain, depression and grief were overwhelming. I was in the 'Fisher divorce seminar.' The information they gave really helped, knowing that people lose friends and that is part of what is normal. Having the group support of others going through the same thing really made a difference."

Connecting Points
Seven Connects to Five

The internal ego states of Five and One are both potential resources for Sevens. In different ways, both counteract the Seven's tendency to pleasure-seek and avoid mundane reality.

The connection to Five offers Sevens a more observant and self-contained life experience. Sevens say they are less extroverted and more reflective in this ego state. Many Sevens say the quiet they find at Five allows them to fill their spiritual reservoir and experience solace in the present. Sevens often discover their creativity is also nurtured by this introversion: "After my divorce I couldn't get a job. I met a farmer who had an apartment in his barn. I was able to work out a deal to take care of his animals in exchange for rent. I played music and lived simply."

However, on the negative side, this quiet and introversion can cause Sevens to become isolated from others. It can also feel disorientating: "I am in this place more these days, but it is frightening. I fear a loss of self, I'll be permanently disabled and lose the core ability to make everyone else happy. My return for making everyone happy is I'll be taken care of. If I renege with my deal with the universe to make everyone happy, then I'll be abandoned." In therapy, this opens rich opportunities to re-think those early "deals."

Seven Connects to One

On the down side of the connection to One, Sevens can be critical, rigid and practice black-and-white thinking. Like Ones, Sevens can be obsessive and perfectionistic. They can be unusually vulnerable to criticism. Sevens can also get caught up in One-like idealism about improving the world to the detriment of attending to their personal needs: "It would be nice if I could let go of saving the world and just focus on making myself a better person. I feel like there isn't enough time to get it all done, and I'm afraid my life will be wasted if I focus only on me."

The up-side of this connection reinforces a Seven's healthy idealism. They are able to set aside their personal desires and focus their attention on making life better for others: "When my wife suggested we move home to care for my dying father I felt a big fear in my chest. Then I knew, it was exactly the right thing to do." Sevens can also express a strong sense of fairness and social justice, which represents a mature aspect of their connection to One.

Dreams

The following dream alludes to the dilemma of a Seven trying to grow: "I am at an amusement park where bizarre stuff is going on. I'm invited for dinner with friends, but I am lost. Desperately lost. I have no shoes on. Strange people are giving me their business cards, because they think I have powers. I'm trying to find a bathroom. I'm going through a house but also a store and a labyrinth. Some parts of the labyrinth go through the house, some through the amusement park, there are rooms with bizarre things going on in them but I just walk by. I missed the dinner party but the experience I was having was so real and bizarre."

Good Enough Therapy

Good enough therapy can help de-construct a Seven client's defensive charm and idealized self and help the Sevens tolerate the truth of his or her feelings. Seven clients need to see through their happy persona and yet appreciate how it kept them safe in the past. When Sevens stop denying large parts of their experience, they open to a wider range of life. When they have access to all their feelings, they open to the depth of who they are. Sober, awake and present they find the real magic that they always sought.

Eights

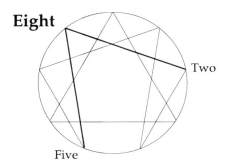

Eight

Two

Five

Presentation in Therapy

- Many Eights have a big energy and a noticeable intensity
- They are usually forthright and direct
- Can play Good Mother or Good Father roles and be protective and nurturing
- May be confrontational and demanding; can readily shift into anger and blame
- Self-referencing; may positively spin their own behavior
- In relationships they can be controlling and sometimes overwhelming
- In conflict, they can seem to have amnesia for their own past behavior; at other times they can be ruthlessly hard on themselves.
- Substance abuse may evolve from excessively enjoying sensory pleasure combined with their need to deny their underlying pain and vulnerability.

Healthy Eights are magnanimous, sharing their power and energy in a community spirit. They are natural leaders who want the best for everybody and act from high ethical values. They are also unguarded, allowing themselves to share the tender side of their heart.

When caught in their unhealthy pattern, Eights can be overpowering and insensitive to others and aggressive about taking what they impulsively desire. They ignore the impact of their bullying behavior on others even as they deny their own vulnerability. The Eight attention style fixes on power, overt control, excess, strength, and justice.

The prevailing American culture has a love affair with the energy of Eights, particularly as a male Archetype. Americans applaud figures like John Wayne or Clint Eastwood playing roles of protective vengeance. Eights say they feel the culture rewards aggression and supports their strong persona: "I never feel like a victim, I'm effective, and I feel society likes this about me." While this is true for both sexes, female Eights often feel pressured to temper their aggression and channel their energy through an acceptable feminine image. It is more common for female Eights to develop the altruism of Two and the introversion of Five (see Connecting Points) at an early age.

Childhood Experiences and Adult Defenses

Eights possess an instinctual sense of truth and the inherent ability to relate to others without prejudice. As children, however, they learn to conceal their openness as they observe a world in which the weak are often victimized and the truth is defined by the most powerful. Those who have power – parents, teachers, authority figures – seem to harmfully misuse it or are too ineffectual to be trusted for protection. Eight children protect themselves by turning up the burner on their instinctual life force. This makes their energy available, abundant, and pleasurable.

Eight children often care for and protect others. As one Eight explained: "Nobody ever stood up for me. I never appeared to need it. I never consciously felt I needed it. It was 100% my job to protect others, and I would stop short of nothing to do it." Another Eight added, "I went and stole a dog from some neighbors who were abusing it. My mom said 'you have to return it.' I said no. I kept it and ran a placement service for other abused animals I found."

The parents of Eights often find it difficult to manage the child's aggressive energy and many Eights remember not feeling held or nurtured: "My mom would tell my dad, 'I cannot handle that kid. You're going to have to do something.'" Some parents respond to the child's power with double messages: "I think my dad liked my aggression even though I got in trouble. Everyone looked to me to solve problems in the neighborhood."

Some Eights remembered throwing their abundant energy into being good students and community leaders. Others were near or over the edge of social approval: "All my life I've been a vicious fighter, always siding with the underdogs and outsiders, always seeing established authority as the enemy; this has been tough in my career because the concept of anyone being my boss is absurd to me."

Some Eights described themselves as having been insecure and even shy, especially as children, but concede that this was probably not how others saw them. Even when conditions caused them to suppress their energy, the importance of being strong and protecting others was constant.

Eights protect themselves with the defense mechanism of *denial,* unconsciously disavowing their thoughts, feeling, wishes, needs or any external facts that are consciously unacceptable. The core neurotic impulse of Eights is "lust" – which can be sexual in nature, but also includes lust for whatever the Eight desires, especially power.

Lust drives Eights to be strong and act on their immediate desires which makes them feel omnipotent. They then deny their weaker feelings and the damaging impact of their actions. By acting quickly and impulsively, Eights avoid reflecting on their behavior, maintaining a momentum that prevents them from recognizing the vulnerability and hurt of others. More importantly this denial keeps them from feeling their own vulnerability. One Eight describes how she would deny her own doubt: "I want to have all my answers right away and I need to show no doubt. Some questions need complexity but I just have an answer in your face, 'That's how I feel, if you don't accept my answer you are wrong.'"

What Brings Eights to Therapy

We often do not see Eights in therapy until they have a major crisis. Their capacity to handle pain without acknowledging it and the reinforcement they get from others for being strong steers them away from self-reflection. The most likely reason for an Eight to seek therapy is the threat of loss of significant others. Someone important to the Eight has "had it" with their behavior and is about to leave: "My wife was leaving me. I had to see how I hurt people 'who matter' and how I had denied the importance of other people's feelings. I deny feeling really bad about hurting people, and this works until people who matter leave." Another Eight added, "I had to give up the belief that it's OK to hurt people."

When the neurotic importance of being in complete control conflicts with relationships, Eights can be blindsided by the feelings that surface: "When I broke up with my first love, it was my first experience with failure. I had always felt in complete charge of my life and I was depressed for the first time. The relationship brought out my softer side. It turns out that relationships are important and I had not realized that."

Other Eights agree that they are the last to know when their "complete control" is an illusion:

• "I was really agitated all the time, denying my emotions about some recent troubles and losses. But, I thought no one could tell. My professor, whom I trusted, asked me 'what my body was telling me?' The question caught my attention, and he referred me to a Gestalt therapist."

• "I just didn't realize what loss really meant until I experienced it."

• "Therapy helped me see that my limitations came from me."

What Does Not Work

Eight clients report that therapists often fail to negotiate their defenses. Eights see through dishonesty easily and, while they do need therapists to be strong, they don't need us to 'act' tough: "It has amused me when therapists try to pick a fight with me in order to see, experience, work with my rage first hand. Any Eight knows when a fight is not real." Eights warn that if they answer a therapist's question too quickly, the therapist should be suspicious: "When a therapist asks me a question that is emotional or thought-provoking, I can clam up. It doesn't mean I don't want to answer. I want to answer in a way that maintains my sense of control. I may give a quick B.S. answer." Therapists who continue to accept "B.S." answers lose the Eight's attention and trust.

Eight clients also say that formulaic approaches that allow them to stay on the surface or require they play a role don't engage them: "For me the least helpful is cognitive therapy. It is just too safe. We can put things together and can stay there. It's fun, I look really good and never get to the vulnerable place. This therapy reinforces staying the same, 'I have it all together and I haven't shared a single wound.'" Another Eight adds: "My wife and I had two sessions with this guy in Chicago, and he was using linguistics, trying to get us to re-state with 'I' messages, etc. I thought right away, 'This is not going to work.' I don't want to waste my time in therapy, I am impatient."

Some Eights may perceive a therapist with a reflective style as too passive or weak: "My first therapist was very quiet. I felt I was overwhelming her. The more I talked the more her eyes got big and she got quiet. I ended up feeling bad, like I had done something wrong." An anxious style is no better: "Later another therapist asked me eager questions like 'Is this helping? I really want to help you.' I got rid of her, too." Eight clients say that therapists should take heed when the Eight asks the therapist questions like: "Are you doing alright?" "Do you understand?" "Are you with me?" If they think the therapist is not strong enough, the Eight may start protecting the therapist by concealing their own needs.

Defended Eights can test and challenge therapists with an impatient, contentious presentation. Some therapists may be intimidated and contract while others could be tempted to adopt a false toughness. Eights warn us that they will read the therapist quickly and give up in disgust if it doesn't look hopeful. The therapy might have had a chance to succeed if the therapists had known how to read the Eight defense and the fear it covers. Here is how Eights say they act when feeling defended in therapy:

• "I test, and challenge you to see if you are willing to be there with me. I need to know."

• "I have spent my whole life with people not getting me. I assume you aren't going to get me either and I come to therapy with a chip on my shoulder."

• "My first thought is: OK, if we have to do this let's make it fast, effective and efficient."

• "Therapists need to understand we will be suspicious and filled with angry denial, and if they can't stand up and fight, we will go elsewhere. You need to understand, we want help more than we will indicate."

What Does Work

Eight clients want the foundations of therapy set as quickly as possible. Most talk of needing a strong, honest, smart therapist with whom they feel safe enough to be vulnerable. Therapists need to know it is hard for Eights to establish trust. Most recommend a forthright approach:

• "Therapy needs to be fast and hard-hitting early on."

• "I need to perceive you have something of power to offer."

• "For the therapist to effectively meet the Eight energy and 'hold the space' they need to be very directive, offering a solid dose of reality."

• "Don't pretend. Tell me the truth."

• "I need someone equal, and intellectually able to handle me."

• "The therapist has to be really intelligent to make me feel safe."

One Eight remembered a therapist who approached her exactly right when she was a smart but troubled teenager: "I was feeling so powerless. First he helped me find answers quickly, which was an intellectual hook. Right away he gave me a Transactional Analysis book and said, 'Here, figure out where you are in the ego blocks section and tell me by the next session.' What I liked so well was that he connected with my mind first and then later he hooked me up with my emotions." The value of first being offered intellectual resources was echoed by another Eight: "The therapist was wonderful. I hadn't realized how I had stuffed my feelings. She gave me information, reading, and assistance with a plan. She kept focus, maintained just the right balance of emotion and direction. She was truthful." When Eights say they want truth, they are asking us to be our most honest; to speak from our most authentic intelligence of body, mind and heart.

During various developmental stages and life crises, having a safe nurturing relationship can be critical for Eights. Teachers and mentors who took an interest in an Eight child can leave a memory of safety and growth through relationship. Therapists can bring the memory of such people into sessions as allies in the current work. An Eight woman remembered a high school teacher who "just took me under her wing. I think she realized I did not fit in and she just spent extra time with me. She was interested in my life and believed in me." This mentoring relationship made a considerable difference: "She believed I was smart and encouraged me to go to college, which I did."

At a different life stage, supportive talk therapy can be exactly the right medicine for an Eight. The same woman above continues: "In college, far away from home for the first time, I became reckless. I drank a lot, was into a lot of sex. I hated my father and was angry.

"I was almost raped and this forced me to look at my omnipotence. I could see this was taking me down a wrong path and I was afraid of failure and looking bad, losing it all. I began to see a counselor, just to let off steam. It was just talk therapy, a safe haven, but it re-directed some of the feelings causing the recklessness. There was no real direction to it but I was in control, came when I wanted to and talked about what I wanted to, it got me through those three years.

"Direction was important later, when therapy empowered me to appreciate my strength and honesty, to be more of an Eight. When I was young I was more shy, I had low self-esteem and withdrew and took care of other people, I let my husband control me. I'm now clear about who I am and I appreciate my passion."

A number of female Eights report relationship histories where they felt controlled. Despite their surface toughness, a surprising percentage had also been victims of physical and verbal abuse.

Contributing factors included the fact that an Eight's strong persona can attract dependent-aggressive men and that some Eights equate fighting with intimacy.

Female Eights can also feel guilty about their own aggression and try to suppress it. They often benefit when therapists help them identify appropriate boundaries and teach them ways to avoid getting caught in their own aggression. Some may fail to protect themselves from present abusive behavior because they haven't forgiven themselves for past relationship failures.

Finding a healthy, powerful feminine identity can be a heroine's journey for Eight women: "I think there are some gender identification issues for female Eights. No way could I have gone to therapy with a woman first. I idealized my father and did not respect my mother. Eventually, though, I needed a woman therapist who could help me know feminine power – that it does not have to be weak."

Family and Conjoint Therapy

One possible dilemma for therapists working with an individual is deciding whether to include other family members in the therapy after individual therapy has begun. Shifting to a conjoint or family context can seem compelling when a client's problems seem more interpersonal than intrapersonal; for example, when the client continually talks about their issues with a significant other.

However, therapists sometimes minimize the risk of betraying the safety of the therapeutic relationship, something Eights are unusually sensitive to: "After about a year in individual therapy for depression my psychiatrist suggested we bring in my (now ex) husband. I went along with it, and it was only for two sessions, but it was like my husband poisoned the space. I just stopped feeling safe.

"I continued with the therapy for another three or four months, but the damage never completely healed. I was far enough along so I quit. I might have done more and deeper work, but we never talked about what it was like for me to have had him there."

An Eight's apparent toughness can belie their actual need for safety. If the therapist thoroughly explores the consequences of inviting another family member into therapy beforehand, it can prevent the client from feeling unsafe or even betrayed. Often it's better for the therapist to refer their Eight client and spouse to another therapist – whose client would be the couple – even if individual work needs to be temporarily put on hold.

In conjoint therapy, Eights can learn to listen and reflect before reacting: "When I get in a disagreement I want to resolve it now. I've learned how to wait."

The language of feelings and vulnerability may be unfamiliar to an Eight client and the therapist may need to make them explicit: "Needs and subtlety just go right over my head. Friends have told me I just do not pick up on clues; when they are needy they have to spell it out or I don't see it." For many Eights, receiving nurturing is equally difficult: "When my partner would try to nurture me it made me angry, brought up feelings of vulnerability. To me it seems black or white. Either no nurturing at all or you open the door to a vulnerability that is bottomless.

"I've been learning it's a matter of degree, but I still sometimes need the other person to spell out what it means. For instance, if my husband says 'I'll take care of you,' it means nothing. If he says 'you can lay in bed for two days and I'll take care of the dogs and feed the kids,' then I know what I can depend on."

Two Eights enthusiastically recommended "Imago Therapy," particularly the 'container' exercise. In this exercise, offered in "Getting the Love You Want" workshops, individuals take turns expressing old angers to their partner.

The technique helped this Eight to break through her anger and allow intimacy: "As a couple we spent 10 days with Harville Hendricks. The approach was very confrontational. It makes you look at your relationship with your parents. I really cried and looked into my sadness. The container exercise allowed me for the first time to have my anger, and it makes you relate this back to childhood. I always felt like my partner could not handle my anger. It allowed me to know that he could handle my anger and gave me parameters around the intensity. I was made responsible for looking in my own self for the causes. Finding out about how to express it, without causing harm. And the vulnerability of asking for what I have never gotten was powerful."

Group therapy can offer Eights support and a sense of community making it safe for them to be vulnerable. At first, however, they may seem to have no needs in a way that belies the actual work they do: "It is hard for me to see how imperfect I am. I had to do this work alone, between group sessions. Otherwise I would have lost too much face. In groups, I have this image of being a leader. When I did finally do some work in my group and even cried, I was amazed to hear others say that they still saw me as strong. They thought I had more guts because of it. I was touched by the group's honesty."

Vulnerability and the Need for Protection

As I said, Eights need more protection in therapy than is readily obvious. One highly experienced couples therapist – herself an Eight – noted that many therapists expect the Eight in a couple to be the one to change. She also finds they push unfairly against the Eight's energy because the Eight seems strong enough to take it. In her own couples counseling, she makes a particular effort to help the Eight's partner understand and decode the Eight's strong reactions, partly because Eights often feel misunderstood.

Several Eights were aware that their abundant energy allowed them to mask the side-effects of substance abuse and high-risk behavior. Therapists may need to look below an Eight client's surface assurances that everything is fine and consider these dangers even if the client won't: "I can be so in control on drugs. I have the energy to use a lot of drugs and still show up and make "A" grades in school and get any job done. I rationalize it by telling myself that I am so intense and that few people can match my intensity. But drugs can match my intensity, making it an attractive 'relationship.' The truth is that Eights are lonely at a core level. We can't express it because we can't admit it. The drugs numb the pain."

Eights say they often neglect themselves and believe they can't depend on anyone else: "By self-definition, I am both un-needful and undeserving of compassion. I need no one's caring." These clients also mask their need for protection with surface toughness towards the therapist. One client described feeling "afraid I was in danger of being dependent on my therapist. She saw me as much stronger than I was. I had a panic attack for the first time ever when I was in therapy with her. I knew this was coming from my fear of the therapy relationship. When I told her I was feeling dependent, she said something about how smart I was, and assured me I was stronger than I thought. She was admiring my defense. I felt shame for my vulnerability, wanted her to hold me, and I was ashamed for even having that thought."

One Eight describes his surprised relief at feeling protected by his therapist: "The first time I ever recall anyone addressing my need for protection was when my therapist – ironically, a tiny, lovely young woman – reacted strongly when I told her about my sexual abuse. She was clearly outraged and angry: 'You were just this beautiful little boy! And you trusted him. Where were your parents? What did they do?' It felt to me as if she had kicked their door down, was holding me by the hand and shaking her finger in their faces. I do not recall ever feeling stood up for, so protected before that. Needless to say, I cried like a baby. With her protecting me, my profound vulnerability could be released and honestly felt. It was an amazing moment. I had no idea I needed that sort of protection."

Working with an Eight client's childhood history depends on the therapist's style as well as the client's interest, need and readiness. Eights can be hyper-sensitive to perceived manipulation and a therapist who acts "too caring" may be suspected of being phony: "If you respond too emotionally I am not giving you any more. It seems manipulative." A therapist's caring may remind Eights of painful buried parts of their history, something they may not be ready to endure. They could also reframe a therapist's empathy as weakness, concluding that the therapist is not strong enough to help them.

When probed, Eight clients often minimize their childhood pain. One Eight suggested trying the following line of inquiry: "Hurting doesn't seem to hurt as much to you as it does to others. Were you ever hurt as a kid?' 'How?'" Making a link between denying their weakness and having been hurt as a child helps Eights recognize present reenactments: "Being angry, hurting others, and denying the importance of feelings protects me from the memory of my own pain."

After the Eight admits their childhood pain, representational objects can remind them to nurture their younger self: "My therapist had me go and buy a doll that looked like me, and she had me go inside and comfort the little girl and the young sexually acting out woman. When I comforted my little girl it made a monumental difference. Sometimes my therapist needed to remind me until I learned to remember to do it myself. She had me bring in a picture of the little girl to see how strong she must have been. I'm in awe of this child."

Working with Denial

Since an Eight's first impulse is to deny their own capacity to hurt others, therapists might have to fish for buried remorse over damage the Eight may have done. One Eight suggested asking a question like: "People hurt people. Have you ever hurt anyone?" Another Eight said, "My therapist holds up a mirror to me and reminds me of old behaviors that I slip into that don't work. For me it's a lot easier just to get mad, leave and forget the bodies I've left in my wake."

When Eights begin to face the damage they may have caused they can get depressed. Both their anger and their passion for life then may seem absent. One Eight who had been through a near divorce advised: "Recognize potential for suicide. The attitude is different from other types. It's 'I did the crime, so I'll do the time.'"

Eights are self-forgetting, which predisposes them to act impulsively in ways they may later regret. One client described how her therapist taught her to visualize her anger instead of acting on it: "I stuff my anger until there is a nasty scene. I'm a scientist so my therapist will start at a scientific level, and break down what happens when I am angry. My heart races, I am crying, my emotions are out of control. This creates pictures, I can see my heart racing, my shortness of breath."

When Eights are impatient and judgmental it often means that their vulnerability is close to their conscious awareness: "Anger is a quick closing of the door against what was about to happen. On this edge Eights are so out of touch with their feelings, except for anger, and so wrapped in denial and so afraid. When a threatening moment comes, along with it comes great risk of being exposed and the weak self being uncovered, the defense is to shut down, to suddenly not give a shit about the process and to deny the moment that had just loomed close and threatening.

"Usually I feel disdain for the whole silly, annoying game of bullshit therapy. There is no point sitting here wasting my time, I'm out of here, fuck this. I've felt it as anger, and as resentment and as not exactly boredom but a sort of tired existential 'why bother?' reaction. I've had two great therapists and in such situations both of them reacted with questions like 'Did you just stop feeling? Where did you go?' or 'You just went away, what were you feeling?' It also helps me to connect my past with my present feelings."

Therapy can give Eights a context for examining the Eight's denial of the guilt and regret they feel about any damage they have caused. It can also help them identify their most authentic intentions, often masked by the aggressive immediacy of their reactions. An Eight described the type of dialogue her therapist effectively used under these circumstances: "I used to give the impression I didn't care, this is not the truth. I would blow someone off in public and I knew I had hurt them, but in private I would play it over and over in my mind, thinking things like 'I can't believe they thought I would do something like that!' Sort of like changing the subject – thinking about what they thought rather than the fact that I had hurt them.

A therapist might ask me: 'So you are saying you can't see how this person's feelings would be hurt?' I would say, 'No I understand they are hurt, but I didn't mean to.' The therapist could then push me further by asking, 'So what did you mean?' I will say anything to stay on top. If you can help me express what I really mean that helps."

Eight clients also remind us to be suspicious of the too-quick answer: "If an Eight answers too fast, the therapist might have to identify that process. He could say something like, 'you are someone who has a quick instinctual answer to most questions and that has worked well for you. But you seem to be ineffective right now in one area of your life. I wonder if you would be open to looking at things in a different way?'"

Converting the Vengeful Mind

An Eight's competitive instinct and discomfort with vulnerability can easily translate into picking on others or be magnified into a sense of vengeance: "Truth is malleable; it feels good to believe whatever makes you feel both strong and justified. But it may lead to hurting others."

One Eight's story illustrates a painful repetition of an unconscious parental triangle: "I still didn't get the integrity piece, I got involved with a colleague's wife for fun, I had made a public comment that I could get this woman from this man and I did. Shortly after he was shot and killed. We all saw it happen, and everyone blamed me even though I had nothing to do with the actual shooting. I moved and brought her with me, but I did not love her. It was guilt. Finally I entered therapy to deal with my depression. The therapist worked with images of the event, making them bigger and smaller. This was NLP and it helped some.

"But the most helpful thing was an exercise where I had to choose five safe people to tell the story to. I thought it was black and white, either I was a really bad person or it didn't matter. Being honest about what I had done and getting a compassionate response allowed me to see my role honestly, forgive myself for the past and change my behavior of playing with people's feelings. I had to look hard at my integrity. I decided I would never casually play with people's feelings again. I also had to understand how my competition with my father and my special role with my mother was part of what had motivated me."

For Eights who are ready to face their habits of harshly judging others, holding themselves exempt and acting vengeful, helping them deconstruct their assumptions is useful: "My therapist asks me think about others and where they are, how to stop and collect myself. She openly talks about how I need to stop and think about the judgments I make about others. She asks me why I make them, how do I know I am right, are they well placed. This makes me break it down and tell the truth. I can be so judgmental and when I get going I don't care if it is true, because it is what I want to believe."

Another Eight added this story: "I went to a spiritual counselor several years ago who said 'You are an incredibly judgmental person, you hurt people with your thoughts, you hurt people with your actions. You might not like their hair, clothes, how they seem to you. But, you need to realize they are somebody's sister, brother or mother – they are *somebody*.'

"Several years went by and I never thought about her words. Then for some reason I did. Since then I've allowed myself to remember her voice as an objective filter. When the hateful thoughts take over I just remember her words. Questioning myself no longer seems like a weakness."

Therapists need to be aware that vengeful thoughts are gatekeepers for deeper feelings that will surface when the Eight's thought-patterns are interrupted: "I've learned to second guess myself. I used to just say whatever I felt like saying. Now I observe how people react to me – with avoidance or fear – and I care about how they feel." Another Eight added, "Learning to be gentle with myself is harder than being vengeful."

When Eights interrupt their lustful vengeful energy, they may feel unmasked and child-like. They can especially benefit from tools that help them heal the innocent child within. Learning to be truthful, while staying compassionate, is the work at this point. Meditations that focus on the heart can be especially helpful.

Connecting Points
Eight Connects to Five

Eights have a connection to Five and to Two. Both help Eights contain their expansive energy, bringing them focus, an objective mindset and an appropriate emotional vulnerability.

Eights express their connection to Five with an attraction to information. Many said, for example, that they needed information to help them tolerate being in therapy. Knowing something about the theories that underly the therapeutic process allows an Eight client a sense of control. "It is important to me," one Eight said, "to have a framework or a container to place myself in. I need to know what is going on. My therapist provided me with background reading material."

Eights also find their Five qualities nurturing and restorative: "Part of my going 100 miles an hour was to avoid quiet, introspection and aloneness. Now I have learned to use the Five part to nurture both myself and others."

On the down side, when Eights are depressed or ashamed of

having lost control in a relationship they can withdraw like a Five, isolating themselves from the support of others. They may then construct self-justifying stories that significantly distort reality and cut them off further. It is helpful for therapists to watch for this tendency and possibly bring it up with the client: "My therapist always confronts me on my tendency to hole up."

Eight Connects to Two

Eights are often caretakers and, like Twos, they can resent giving too much, especially to those who don't seem to help themselves. They may, however, feel codependently compelled to fight other people's battles: "I always have vengeful thoughts, but if I act on them I feel awful. Still, other people want me to act on them and sometimes I get used."

One Eight said that her therapist helped her manage her caretaking tendencies by continually asking: "Who are you *really* protecting?" and "Why are you protecting *them*?" These questions helped the Eight see how she projected her own needs and childhood wounds. For Eights, finding a balance between protecting those who seem defenseless versus slamming the door on giving can be a rich source of growth.

On the high side, developing their inner Two helps Eights express their compassion and big hearts. An Eight therapist said: "I have a quick and very accurate intuitive reading of people, and can almost feel what is hurting them, and what they need from me."

Dreams

Many Eights report dreams that are vivid, fast, dramatic and colorful. One Eight woman remembered a recurrent dream from high school, a time when she did not 'fit in': "I had these school bus dreams. I always had a green hat on. I hate hats and I hate green. Typically the bus was out of control; there was usually something wrong with the driver. The bus had big windows, I saw things outside going by really fast. I sat in the seat with my stupid green hat on. Things are going by and I have to take control. Finally I do something – either drive the bus myself or stop it somehow."

Had this dreamer been in therapy her therapist might have learned a great deal from her dreams, perhaps about her struggles with undependable adults, or her unstable sense of being out of control and looking for a way out. Perhaps she knew was going to have to grow up fast in order to survive. Dreams can cut through an Eight's denial.

Good Enough Therapy

An Eight's therapist should meet their client's tough defense with honesty and authentic strength. They may also need to offer solid information delivered with compassion and competency. The Eight client's denial needs to be skillfully confronted. As Eights recognize the damage done by the momentum of their aggression, they need a therapist to stay truthful, but also help the Eight alter, understand and forgive their own behavior. The therapist may also have to extend a protective quality when an Eight's vulnerable self – no longer masked by denial – begins to emerge. The path of growth for Eights is to remember their quality of innocence and integrate it as a rightful aspect of their true strength.

Nines

Nine

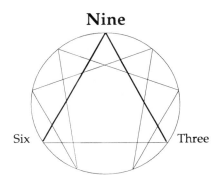

Six   Three

Presentation in Therapy
- Nines can be easygoing, pleasant, passive and agreeable
- Some have difficulty making decisions and defining their opinions
- May speak in"sagas" that are sometimes entertaining and sometimes dull; can offer inessential details that sidetrack therapy
- If relationship issues prompt therapy, the Nine may appear distant and passive; the spouse and family members may be very angry
- They can have a diffuse energy and respond slowly
- Difficulty identifying their own needs and feelings; focus on others, including the therapist
- May use indirect angry humor and exhibit passive-aggressive behavior
- Substance abuse may develop as a way to numb feelings that might lead to conflict. It can also release suppressed feelings and thoughts that make Nines act uncharacteristically combative and provocative.

At their best, Nines harmoniously connect with others in a way that allows everyone to feel valued. They do this without losing sight of their own contribution and importance.

When caught in their unhealthy pattern, Nines merge with others and lose their sense of self. They feel angry at being overlooked but mask it by being agreeable. Their anger comes out in passive-aggressive ways; by not following through, letting others down in a disengaged, even pleasant style. The Nine attention fixes on finding peace and comfort, identifying with all points of view and avoiding conflict.

American culture rewards ambitious and competitive behavior. Individuals who are articulate and definite about their interests are thought of as intelligent, strong and possibly leaders. Nines, who tend to seek consensus and can be passive about fulfilling personal goals, can be devalued and seen as weak. Nine women, on the other hand, may merge with traditional female roles and be accepted by the culture, even to their own detriment.

Childhood Experiences and Adult Defenses

As children, Nines are innately clear about what matters to them while being sensitive to other people's feelings. But, they often perceive their family environment as a place where they have to choose between being themselves and being connected to others. The Nine child fears that if their personal desires differ from those important in their lives – especially parents – it will lead to separation and loss. The child resolves this double-bind by forgetting his or her true self and pretending to want what others want. While Nines are naturally empathetic, they can lapse into defensive merging. They then distract themselves from their personal priorities and needs, inducing in themselves a sleepy, unfocused approach to life.

Nines describe the experience of merging as a warm confluence between their body and another's. It is as though the Nine only exists to mirror others. When they report their family history, they can, for instance, slip into recounting the life of another family member instead of their own.

In a Genogram, Nines can appear as the classic lost child, or the "no problem" child, or the child whose troubles are due to following a peer group. Nines who are asleep to their sense of industry often achieve less in life than they have potential for. The exception is when a Nine has merged with someone who is aggressive and highly motivated.

Nines ward off awareness of their lost self with the defense mechanism of *narcotization* often referred to as "numbing out." Depending on the individual, this defense can manifest as overeating, watching TV excessively, creating pointless busy work, daydreaming or getting lost in fantasy. Any inessential activity that drains energy from a Nine can keep them from being present and awake to their own desires and needs.

In Enneagram books this is called *sloth*, although the term is misleading because Nines can be very active and productive. They may still, however, be asleep to what is important to them. Nines avoid "wakefulness" because becoming aware of their own priorities could provoke conflict and rejection. One Nine explained: "I would play a computer game, thinking 'just for a couple of minutes,' before writing a report. I would not realize I had been playing it for two or three hours, during which time I was unaware of what was going on around me or what was important. I would have forgotten the reason I was going to the computer in the first place was to write a report, and I would be past the deadline for getting it done. I finally had to delete all the games from the computer."

What Brings Nines to Therapy

In my survey, I found many Nines who had experienced psychotherapy. They most often sought help for relationship conflicts, depression, anxiety and angst about life direction. The Nine's tendency to sacrifice their own priorities over time generates anger, resentment, and a deep sadness.

Nines fear that getting angry will lead to separation and loss so they express their anger passive-aggressively, through mean jokes, sideways comments, or by not listening. Other indicators of anger might be: agreeing to do things but not doing them, or becoming stubborn and uncommunicative. In couples work, the Nine's partner could be overtly angry while the Nine appears amiable and a bit bewildered. Like any person who passively refuses to take responsibility for their emotions, Nines can mysteriously stir them up in others.

What Does Not Work

Therapists who want to intervene skillfully with Nines may be challenged by the way they can deflect, deny, or forget important emotional content. Nines can play out this pattern in their relationships by allowing themselves to be overlooked, failing to communicate their thoughts and feelings and or even recognize them until it is too late. Later, they suddenly awaken to feelings of overwhelming resentment. They can act out this pattern with a therapist as well.

Tom Condon has described Nines as presenting therapists with an "amiable defeatism." Previous therapy may have failed them and they may assume that any new attempts will also fail. Condon suggests that therapists ask their Nine clients what has *not* worked in the past as a way to predict the probable transference/counter-transference. The client's answer could help the therapist make an effective treatment plan that avoids repeating previous mistakes. It also helps Nines to hear their own story and observe their own patterns. This question, of course, could work with any type.

Some Nine clients need to be evaluated more carefully: "Over the years I've worked with about eight different psychotherapists, typically over a period of a few months each. My experience has been uniformly negative. After a few weeks of therapy – the "getting to know you" phase – the therapist begins to challenge my beliefs. Eventually, I give up and quit therapy. What I would like from psychotherapy is to feel optimistic, competent, and 'OK,' rather than feeling like an emotional mess." Not surprisingly, this informant reported finding more help from personal growth workshops, which supported his immediate goals of feeling optimistic and competent.

Given this client's history with therapy, asking what had not worked in the past could prevent another treatment failure. But, a therapist might also need to explain to him what therapy is and is not. It would be good to encourage this client to go to personal growth workshops, which offer refuge in the positive without the emotional risks of therapy. Later, he could be ready for the kind of change therapy can provide.

Many Nines unconsciously believe that they cannot have what they want, so fear of failing in therapy can be deep and potent. A therapist working with a Nine could seem to stir up a great deal of therapeutic insight. The client appears to make a breakthrough in the session, yet no action follows. Nines can banish therapeutic insights from their awareness or memory, especially if they threaten the Nine's core survival strategy. The therapist thinks she is getting to deep issues while the Nine unconsciously feels threatened. Therapists often feel confused and thwarted by this recurring mind-set.

On the plus side, Nines are almost always pleasant people who are willing to explore a problem. They are genuinely forgiving as well, especially when someone makes a real effort to understand them, a gesture they may find therapeutic in itself.

Nines said that therapy failed them in two ways: (1) When therapists did not sufficiently challenge them to face their anger and avoidance or (2) when the therapist became too "helpful."

On the one hand, the therapy hour can slip into being just another place for the Nine client to go to sleep:

- "I wish psychotherapists would realize that what I need, as a

Nine, is to start taking action and responsibility for my life, rather than waiting for something to 'just happen.' It's too easy for me to ignore problems and hope they just go away."
- "You can go over things in therapy, and it becomes ritualized, with no progress."
- "Insight alone is not going to help."

On the other hand, Nine clients need to be confronted, albeit at a slow pace. If you rush them they tend to give up. Several Nines reported feeling pressured and misjudged by therapists who "pushed too hard and fast, demanding assertiveness." The clients insisted they were willing to work at therapy, but needed to proceed at their own speed.

Therapists working with Nines should be mindful of any expectations they have that the client will change. A Nine can offer a passive receptiveness that some therapists take as an invitation to offer solutions. A therapist who begins to make helpful suggestions, but fails to uncover what the Nine really wants, is baiting a hook that will lead to discouragement. Some Nines who appear interested and agreeable are just reading what the therapist wants in the moment. This can lead to a transference/counter-transference dynamic where the client seems to be trying but fails to change, disappointing the therapist. The client then feels bad about his or her self and begins to resent the therapist.

A therapist who does not recognize this counter-transference can easily begin setting goals for the Nine, goals which the Nine will subtly oppose. The therapist is now attached to an outcome and the Nine is angry. But the therapist might not know it; the therapy just seems to go sour.

Since Nines specialize in making people feel good, good feelings may not indicate good work. To keep sessions moving forward, a therapist may need to honestly identify any counter-transference and evaluate the reality of the Nine's good feelings. The therapist might play Devil's Advocate by saying things like: "It seems like you're going along with this, but I'm wondering if this is *really* working for you."

A Nine client could also make the therapist the problem: "My therapist just seemed to get stuck on the idea that I had to leave my husband. She wouldn't drop it and seemed disgusted at the choice I was making." The therapist in question was an experienced psychodynamic psychologist working with a client who was passively choosing to stay with her spouse. He had recently admitted molesting her now-adult children and was now refusing treatment. Although the Nine had entered therapy to work on the abuse, her anger was clearly focused on the therapist. Her reaction was an example of *displacement* – unconsciously redirecting her emotions from their original source to a more acceptable subject.

A therapist might suspect displacement if a subtle power struggle gradually develops over time. The Nine client may leave sessions increasingly discouraged and disgruntled yet never openly express their dissatisfaction. For real change to occur, Nines need to identify their own issues and take charge of their own problem solving; in effect creating and following their own treatment plan: "If I have ownership of something and have thought of it myself, then I want to carry through with it."

Nines are naturally compassionate and intuitive about the needs of others. In therapy, they can slip into taking care of the therapist's needs while avoiding their own work. They are often warm and funny and present in a social, conversational manner that can bypass their real pain: "I was going through a divorce, in a lot of pain at home and using substances, but I didn't talk about any of that with the therapist. I could snow the therapist easily. I could see what he would see as healthy and would present that to him, present an 'I've got it together' image. I also could sense the therapist was a little rushed. Everyone knows they are overworked; I did not want to take too much of his time."

Sadly, this fits the Nine's childhood experience of not wanting to be a problem or call attention to their personal needs. When I asked this client what the therapist could have done differently, he replied: "He could have asked me more questions like 'What are you doing with your grief over this divorce?' Or: 'What is it like to be here now in therapy?' I would have liked it if he had kept me focused by probing, staying with my issues, and perhaps doing a family history to give me insights into prior losses."

As they do with other people, Nines will try to create a harmonious relationship with the therapist by merging with them: "Harmony is *so* easy to slip into." Ironically, this is what probably brought them to therapy to begin with. Nines tell us that it might be difficult to spot their defense because they are so talented at making others comfortable – which is their defense:

- "I would merge with the therapist so she would feel comfortable so I would be comfortable."
- "I tend to go along with what the therapist wants – like if they make a suggestion. But I probably would not follow through on their

suggestions."
- "I might talk about things other than myself like just something inessential – just try to maintain that comfort level."

In response to a Nine client's passive distracting presentation, the therapist may feel angry, frustrated, or protective. He or she could also feel sleepy, distracted, bored or overly comfortable.

What Does Work

Nines who are caught in their pattern tend to ruminate about their own problems from a passive observer's perspective, meanwhile taking no responsibility or corrective action. Several Nines I spoke with advised therapists to encourage them, help them set goals for therapy, provide suggestions for homework, but remain detached from any outcome. The following approaches take advantage of the Nine's innate creative resources, while keeping the responsibility in their hands.

Brainstorming and Visualizing Virtual Realities

It is often valuable to help Nines learn *future forecasting*, a technique used in mediation in which someone imagines and then experientially "tries on" various possible futures from the safety of the present. First, the therapist helps the Nine client imagine all possible outcomes of a particular situation, including what will happen if no action is taken. The therapist guides the client to develop a full sensory experience of the various futures, making them as real as possible including physical sensations and corresponding emotions.

This technique makes use of the fact that Nines often know what they don't want. It helps them get in touch with the negative future in store for them if they continue on the path of least resistance. In addition, they may also have new insights into past behaviors and their consequences as well as realize their central role in shaping their own destiny. The therapist can then ask questions like: "So where would you like to go instead?" Nine clients often feel energized and come up with their own plan.

In their book, *Narrative Means to Therapeutic Ends*, Michael White and David Epston teach a method they call "Imagining Unique Outcomes," which nicely follows on future forecasting. White and Epston point out that people select memories that support the stories and themes they live now. Therefore, people who see themselves as having problems identify with stories that support that view. By asking questions about the client's history, the therapist can unearth alternative stories that highlight the client's strengths. If a Nine's dominate story is that they never get what they want, the therapist would help them find examples in their past when they pursued what they wanted and got it. The therapist could follow up with more questions like: "How did you get to be so clear about what you wanted this occasion?" and "What does this say about you as a person?" As the client integrates these alternative stories into her present story, she begins to imagine better future outcomes.

A therapist might also help Nines remember times when they felt deeply alive, times of exceptional emotional range and richness. This gets them in touch with the subjective difference between being comfortably numb versus something better. One Nine said it is "especially exciting to me when I am asked what I'm *passionate* about rather than just what do I want." Another Nine began to challenge his acceptance of what he called "mediocrity in the service of harmony."

A related method that works well is to have Nine clients close their eyes and visualize the old woman or old man they will become. The old person is then invited to consult with and advise the Nine client about the negative or positive potential of a present course of action. This older version of the Nine, who lives with the consequences of current behavior, has useful information about the action's likely outcome. Other parts of the client's personality, including a younger self, can also be brought into the exercise to form a kind of committee. Once the Nine has a sense of their different selves, they can continue the conversation through journaling. This exercise usually leads Nines to more self-awareness, a clearer sense of what is important to them and further motivation to take charge of their life.

One Nine said "Nines are like water following the path of least resistance. Consequently, we often aren't recognized or noticed." Nines commonly feel unseen and it helps to guide them towards making themselves more visible. One way to do this is to teach them to observe themselves from other people's point of view. One Nine I worked with felt she was not being heard by her partner whenever there was conflict. First I asked her to visualize herself looking at her partner during the conflict. Then I had her float over and assume her partner's view, to see herself through her partner's eyes. From this vantage point, she saw herself acting agreeable and revealing little. Following this insight she began to communicate what she really felt. Therapists also help Nines see themselves when they "point out the valuable contributions that are unique and appreciated and encourage me to hear the positives about myself."

Nines appreciate therapists who offer sympathetic support, cognitive insight and focus: "Therapy helped me to not feel guilty about defending my position in conflict. Now when it's done, it's done. My therapist helped me recognize the consequences of going along with what I don't want. She helped me see my own perspective." One Nine said that when therapy got uncomfortable, he "bailed out or got numb." His therapist then pressed on with more questions: "She was persistent, rephrased her questions, and asked again in a less direct way. She kept at it to get more clear." One Nine needed a therapist to "Help me remember. Don't forget what I've said. I do enough of that myself."

Another Nine said, "When my self-forgetting starts to emerge, my therapist will say: 'Is there something you aren't talking about today that maybe you need to?' This helps me to check in with myself or she asks, 'What else can I be helpful with today?' I can't merge with her; she has no agenda for me, and I have to search for my own. She supports my agenda when I find it." Another Nine said his therapist asked: "What is it like to have the focus on you?" Nines often find it awkward and difficult to be the center of attention and this can be a helpful area to explore.

Nines said that their most helpful therapists stayed obviously interested in them, but were unattached to a therapeutic outcome. If a Nine client brings up something they want in their life – say applying to graduate school – the therapist might ask the Nine if the client wants to set a deadline. This can help clarify for the Nine what they really do want, versus what they may hypothetically want, or believe the therapist wants them to want. The therapist could also double-check by asking, "I wonder if you are pleasing me or if you really want this for yourself?" As one Nine also added: "If I trust the therapist and if the seed of what I want is established, the therapist could help by asking me, 'How could you sabotage this?' This is particularly good if I have talked in previous sessions about the ways I have sabotaged what I wanted."

Journaling and Self Observation
Many Nines said that keeping a journal was an especially useful adjunct to therapy. Writing about their daily experiences helped them notice when and how they forgot themselves. They could also better distinguish between their own feelings and those of others. Nine clients also discovered more about how they avoided conflict, unconsciously opposed or protected others versus speaking their own truth. Journaling supports such self-observing and can help it become

a habit.

Writing about their thoughts, feelings and experiences also helps Nines strengthen their sense of what matters to them. As Nines endure the discomfort that comes with self-awareness and self-disclosure they often find the courage to speak their truth.

When Nines get in touch with what matters most to them, it may stir up anxiety. They may be afraid that admitting what they want will cause conflict and loss. A therapist can help assuage this anxiety by reassuring the client that 'just the practice of noticing is sufficient, no action needs to be taken.' As the client becomes more congruent with their own desires and works through their fear, they will often spontaneously begin to take positive action on their own behalf.

Journaling also helps clients clarify their part in interpersonal conflicts. One Nine reported that, when she was feeling resentful in relationships, journaling gave her insight into what preceded her passive-aggressive behavior. She realized when she skipped meetings or failed to complete agreed-upon tasks she actually felt resentful: "Writing about it helped me remember that I didn't think about what I wanted when I agreed, I just wanted to please the other person. Now I'm starting to observe my feelings before I agree, avoiding my tendency to give myself away, which leads to resentment and low self-esteem. I am now getting better at learning to communicate what I mean."

Not all Nines are comfortable with writing, but creative variations are possible. One Nine disliked writing, but enjoyed painting and drawing. Her therapist asked her to keep a journal in which she drew her thoughts and feelings using her non-dominate hand.

Feeling Grief

Therapists can help Nines track their tendency to forget themselves back to its childhood origins. As mentioned, Nine children often believed that other people's feelings were more important so they tried to be "good" by hiding their pain and anger. One Nine called this her "parental merge," explaining that "needing parental approval got to be a life or death situation. So I merged with whatever they wanted."

As Nines remember their childhood they often get in touch with the sadness and loss they felt. One client said, "My therapist met my childhood grief with understanding, empathy, and patience. Even so, it took a long time for me to recover a sense of myself."

Many Nines say that a therapeutic relationship where they are treated as valuable and important is itself curative. One Nine recalled a therapist who revealed that she had been diagnosed with cancer. Throughout the therapy the therapist kept the Nine informed about the status of her health, while reassuring her she would not abandon her. The client felt honored that the therapist would confide in her during such a difficult time.

Conjoint Work

In couples therapy, Nines recommend that therapists pay close attention to their non-verbal cues. Since Nines merge with others they can seem invisible when other family members are present. A Nine woman in an emotionally abusive relationship described how this felt: "The therapist failed to recognize what my merging with my husband was costing me. The therapist did not seem to think my needs were important." Asked how the therapist would know if she felt overlooked, this woman replied, "My eye contact stops. I don't nod my head." Other Nines agreed that these were signs that this woman had given up on the therapy. The therapist might have become sleepy, unfocused and complacent, a common counter-transference when working with Nines.

Another Nine remembered working with a marriage counselor who suggested that he not look at or touch his wife when he told her how he felt. Doing this allowed him to stay clear and honest about his own feelings. It interrupted his habit of saying what he thought she wanted to hear, since he was unable to read her non-verbal cues and assess her reaction. In the same way, some Nines find solitude helpful for discerning what is important to them: "When I spend time by myself I start to separate from the energy of others."

Recognizing and Expressing Anger

Anger is at the core of a Nine's personality, and yet Nines often do not seem outwardly angry: "My usual response to a stressful situation is to space out. When I'm in a psychotherapy session, I force myself to engage with the therapist, which results in my feeling angry. For me, anger is a very unpleasant feeling, and after each therapy session, I soon drop back into a kind of spaced-out depression." Another Nine added, "In couples therapy, I was not allowed to express anger; this is the main reason the therapy failed. The therapist could have helped by encouraging acceptable expressions of my deep and long-held anger."

Several Nines recommended that therapists use methods that help them to be aware of their body "because when I'm in my body I'm not spaced out." These included: Reichian therapy, Hakomi, and techniques employing breath work and sound.

In a therapeutic approach called PAIRS, which seems to use psychodrama, a Nine male described being helpfully pushed where he didn't want to go: "The men were together and each was taken to an emotional place that fit for them. When it was my turn I was not emotional. I was lying on the ground; the therapist was a little provocative, asking a repeating question about power, encouraging me to stay in my body. The other men pushed me against the wall until I had to push back. Doing so filled me with power and vitality. I pushed back the entire group to reclaim my space. In the end I went to each man and said 'I am a powerful person.' As a male, being provoked from a male socialization point of view was useful, given the foundation of trust."

This same man summarized what he learned: "When I stuff my anger I lose touch with all my other emotions as well. When I take the risks to say how I feel, it may cause conflict in the short run. But in the long run my life has been richer."

Another Nine client who complained of feeling like a "terrible person" whenever she was angry said her therapist asked reality checking questions. For example, the Nine was asked, "Why is it bad that you don't want to take a salad to your sister's party?"... "Because I love my sister"... "And why does it mean that you don't love your sister if you don't..." By getting more and more specific, the therapist helped the Nine untangle what she really meant when she called herself a "terrible person."

Her therapist had also suggested that she "let her anger be her guide." She tried to be more alert to times when she might be angry. For example, upon re-reading her journals she discovered sarcastic passages and instances where she wrote with what she called "sideways irony." This in turn helped her notice times in daily life when she was angry – *before* she said yes when she wanted to say no. She also realized that sometimes when she felt ill, especially in her abdomen, she was actually feeling angry.

After Nines admit to being angry in specific instances, they can begin to acknowledge the feeling's presence more generally. Many Nines say it is both exciting and frightening to realize how much anger is a part of their unrecognized self. They are also relieved to discover that it is useful, a royal road to right action. The Nine above, for instance, added: "Being given permission to have my monsters and work with them, asking myself 'why this monster is speaking to me right now' has really made a difference. I'm much clearer about my motives."

Once Nines learn about and claim their anger, the next step is to work through their attendant grief about having given up their own priorities. If this work is effective they will usually continue to stay awake to themselves. Working through their grief gives Nines the focus, clarity and initiative to act on what matters most to them. To paraphrase Victor Frankel, they awaken to the obligations that arise out of the responsibility of their being.

Connecting Points
Nine Connects to Three
Nines have a connection to both the high and low side of Three. On the high side, the Three connection helps Nines get in touch with what author David Daniels calls their "healthy narcissism." One client explained: "I need a therapist to help me plant seeds. If I know that something I want is attainable, I will go after it. I need to stew on the positive possibility. So often I get in touch with my Six energy and stew on the negative possibility." Another Nine said it helped him to consistently encourage himself by writing down little sayings like 'seize the moment' and 'go for it' as reminders.

A therapist working with this Three connection might ask a Nine: "What would it be like if you really went after what you wanted and got it?" This question could evoke memories where the Nine felt unsafe about wanting anything – good material to work with. The next question might be: "What would it be like if you *continued* to get what you want?" This might stir up further inhibitions or lead to a positive plan.

On the down side of their connection to Three, Nines will occasionally act out with uncharacteristic bursts of attention-getting behavior, grabbing the spotlight and over-running others. It is as though the need to be special leaps out of the shadows and momentarily takes the Nine over. This behavior is quickly forgotten if no one notices, but if someone reacts badly the Nine feels embarrassed. If a Nine can learn about and accept their connection to Three, they can accept their need to be important and respected and can learn to give it to themselves. They then express the need with grace and maturity as well as obtain better outcomes. They also become more motivated and positive in their outlook as is typical of Threes.

Nine Connects to Six
Nines also have a connection to the up and down side of Six. The down side brings an agitated general anxiety, which Nines feel as a

need to keep moving; sitting still is difficult and their thoughts can be jumbled or even paranoid.

While this anxious state feels negative to Nines, it has the advantage of making them so uncomfortable that they are willing to face things they would otherwise avoid. This is a great time for a therapist to push the edge by recommending practices like meditation and journaling as well as focusing on what surfaces when the client feels this way.

This kind of existential anxiety also interrupts a Nine's inertia and ignites the courage to move beyond their passive "peace at any price" stance. In addition, they develop higher self-esteem, more access to their emotions and a sense of hope for themselves. Intuition, faith, loyalty and spontaneous humor are all aspects of the Nine's inner connection to Six.

Dreams

Paying attention to dreams also helps Nines awaken to what they want. One client who was experiencing a stretch of sleepiness shared the following dream sequence:

"I am on death row and strangely I don't seem disturbed. Tim Robbins, the actor, is very upset on my behalf. He is writing letters and making an emotional appeal to save my life. Three uniformed men later walk me down a long hallway. Unconcerned, I am taken to a room and given something to drink. As I drink, I begin to lose consciousness; I know I am dying." This dream, which the dreamer found interesting, but not unsettling, was followed within days by another: "I am with a type Six friend whom I care about deeply. She has had a difficult life and is often suicidal. We are to take my beloved dog to be put to sleep. He is healthy and I wonder if it is too soon. We go to a veterinarian's office, and the receptionist cheerfully says, 'Sure, we can do it this afternoon.' Then I wake up sobbing."

The order of these dreams illustrates how the unconscious tries to get the dreamer's attention by producing ever more potent symbols. Keeping a dream journal is especially recommended as another way for Nines to continue to listen to themselves.

Good Enough Therapy

By staying interested, compassionate and unattached, therapists can empower Nines to embrace what is most important to them. When Nines awaken to their true self they claim all their personal feelings including anger. As Nines learn to accept the necessity for conflict they discover it actually improves relationships and leads to more authentic union with others – one of their primary motivations. Therapy with Nines often involves resolving grief over their loss of self. Nines ultimately learn they can use their empathic gift of understanding and caring for others, while honoring and acting upon what is important to them.

Appendices:
Resources and Recommendations

Good books for learning about the Enneagram:

Almaas, A.H. *Facets of Unity, the Enneagram of Holy Ideas* (Diamond Books, 1998). The founder of the Diamond Heart School explores the spiritual basis of the Enneagram and the "holy ideas" of each type.

Bast, Mary and Thomson, Clarence, *Out of the Box: Coaching with the Enneagram* (Portland, Oregon: The Enneagram Consortium Press, 2004). Applies Enneagram insights for personal change in coaching. Highly useful for coaches, business people as well as therapists and counselors.

Condon, Thomas, The Dynamic Enneagram: *How to Work with Your Personality Style to Truly Grow and Change* (Portland, Oregon: The Enneagram Consortium, 2004). A comprehensive resource for applying the Enneagram to changework from the perspective of a master hypnotherapist and teacher.

Empereur, James, *The Enneagram and Spiritual Direction: Nine Paths to Spiritual Guidance* (The Continuum International Publishing Group, 1997). Presents a model for spiritual growth within an Enneagram framework, with insights applicable to therapy.

Enneagram Monthly. A journal that includes articles, interviews with well-known Enneagram teachers and thinkers, news, book/movie/workshop reviews, teaching schedules. To subscribe call (650) 851-3113.. Website at http://www.ideodynamic.com/enneagram-monthly/

Daniels, David, M. D. and Price, Virginia, Ph.D, *The Essential Enneagram: The Definitive Personality Test and Self-Discovery Guide* (San Francisco: HarperSanFrancisco, 2000). This small book includes a test for self-typing, minimizing clinical time spent on assessment. The material and presentation are accessible and professional.

Keyes, Margaret Frings, *Emotions and the Enneagram: Working Through Your Shadow Life Script* (Molysdatur Publications, 1992). Filters the Enneagram through Jungian psychology. Offers specific recommendations for personal growth.

Maitri, Sandra, *The Spiritual Dimension of the Enneagram* (New York: Putnam, 2000). An excellent source of spiritual insight. Sandra Maitri is an Enneagram teacher with the Diamond Heart School.

Naranjo, Claudio, M.D., *Character and Neurosis, an Integrative View* (Nevada City, CA: Gateways/IDHHB, Inc., 1994). The first clinical application of the Enneagram, presented in the language of ego psychology and psychotherapy. Applies theory from Oscar Ichazo, Karen Horney and others.

Naranjo, Claudio, M.D., *Enneatypes in Psychotherapy* (Prescott, AZ: Hohm Press, 1997). Excerpts from a conference with therapists, with an emphasis on transference biases and subtypes.

Riso, Don and Hudson, Russ, *The Wisdom of the Enneagram: The Complete Guide to Psychological and Spiritual Growth for the Nine Personality Types* (New York: Bantam, 1999). This popular book is a fine resource for anyone using the Enneagram for personal growth and spiritual transformation.

Rohr, Richard, *Discovering the Enneagram* New York: Crossroads Publishing Company, 1997). Richard Rohr is a Catholic priest who writes about the Enneagram from the perspective of contemplative Christianity. He has several Enneagram books, all insightful.

Schwartz, Tony, *What Really Matters* (New York: Bantam, 1995). A short history of the human potential movement told through the author's personal experience. Includes overviews of the major schools and interviews with teachers. Profiles Helen Palmer and details the modern history of the Enneagram.

Thomson, Clarence and Condon, Thomas, *Enneagram Applications: Personality Styles in Business, Therapy, Medicine, Spirituality and Daily Life* (Portland, Oregon: The Enneagram Consortium, 2001). An anthology of articles about the many ways the Enneagram is being personally and professionally applied. First in a series.

Wagele, Elizabeth and Baron, Renee, *The Enneagram Made Easy* (San Francisco: Harper SanFrancisco, 1994). An accessible and fun book illustrated with cartoons. I give it to teenagers for self-assessment, but it is great for anyone.

Wagele, Elizabeth, *The Enneagram of Parenting* (New York: Harper Collins, 1997). Quick descriptions of the behavior and needs of children with different Enneagram styles. This book gives basic suggestions for understanding and communicating with children at their level of development and avoiding labels. Cartooned for tired parents.

Zuercher, Suzanne, O.S.B., *Enneagram Spirituality* (Ave Maria Press, 1992). Explores the Enneagram and spiritual growth from a Christian perspective.

The Enneagram in Relationships:

The Enneagram is especially useful interpersonally. Good resources include:

Goldberg, Michael, *The 9 Ways of Working* (New York, NY: Marlowe & Co., 1999). An entertaining, intelligent book about the Enneagram at work. Goldberg gives vivid examples of each Enneagram style, suggestions for growth and a directory of how each style interacts with other styles.

Palmer, Helen, *The Enneagram in Love and Work* (New York: HarperCollins, 1995). One of several good Enneagram books by Palmer. This one includes a relationship directory that is both accurate and helpful. I use it as a reference and recommend it to clients trying to understand their role in relationships.

Wagele, Elizabeth and Baron, Renee, *Are You My Type, Am I Yours?* (San Francisco: HarperSanFrancisco, 1995). Easy reading, cartoon illustrations. Looks at both relationships and subtypes.

The Enneagram in Movies, Literature and Biography

One of the most enjoyable ways to learn about Enneagram character styles is through movies, literature and biography. Good resources include:

Condon, Thomas, *The Enneagram Movie and Video Guide* (Portland, Oregon: The Enneagram Consortium, 1999). The consistency of Enneagram styles in movie characters also validates the accuracy of the system. In an enjoyable writing style, Tom Condon reviews hundreds of movies that reveal Enneagram styles.

Searle, Judith, *The Literary Enneagram, Characters from the Inside Out* (Portland, Oregon: The Enneagram Consortium, 2001). An insightful book from a literary scholar and Enneagram expert. Readers who love story and character development, which would include most therapists, will find this a treasure.

Zuercher, Suzanne, O.S.B., *Merton, An Enneagram Profile* (Ave Maria Press, 1996). A biographical study of an Enneagram Four, the famous contemplative and social activist Thomas Merton.

Beyond Books

One dynamic way to learn about the Enneagram is by watching live "panel" presentations, where a teacher interviews groups of people with the same Enneagram style. This approach – taught by Helen

Palmer who calls it the "Narrative Tradition" – is fascinating for how it illuminates both the similarities and the differences in people with the same Enneagram style. Audience members can ask questions of the panelists, deepening their understanding of the Enneagram and bringing the styles alive.

Panels are a great resource for both therapists and their clients. A directory of Oral Tradition teachers is available at: http:// www.authenticenneagram.com. They also offer several excellent videotapes as does Enneagram teacher Julie Foster (415-383-8138). Her email address is: coloradoenneagrm@aol.com.

Note: Panels conducted by therapists that include their clients present some obvious ethical gray areas. However, when clients are fully briefed on the limits of confidentiality in a semi-public milieu, and transference/counter-transference issues have been addressed, participating on a panel can enhance the client's therapy.

Subtypes and Wings

Two important distinctions in the Enneagram model, *wings* and *subtypes*, are not included in this book.

The *wings* refer to the neighboring styles on either side of someone's core Enneagram style. A Four, for instance, could have a Three wing or a Five wing. While most people identify with one wing, both are influential and shade the expression of a person's core Enneagram style.

Subtypes refer to subtle habits of attention devoted to three areas of life – self-preservation, intimate relationships and social standing. Someone's subtype will channel their attention and further skew how they express their core Enneagram style. Many people favor one subtype although the others are unconsciously present. When one subtype predominates it is often to compensate for developmental stress.

Both subtypes and wings are highly recomended areas of study as they both reveal keys for change. The influence of each can alter the inner experience and the outer appearance of an individual, and they greatly add to the Enneagram's richness as a diagnostic model.

Good resources include:

Experiencing Enneagram Subtypes by Julie Foster is a videotape series of subtype panels that enable the viewer to see and hear the subtle differences in the subtypes. To purchase call 415-383-8138 or email: coloradoenneagrm@aol.com.

The Enneagram's Subtypes: the Subtle Drivers of Unconscious Behavior by Tom Condon is an audio CD set, edited from a live workshop. He has another another CD set about wings as well as a series of videotapes. Available through The Changeworks, P.O. Box 5909, Bend, OR 97708-5909. Call: 541-382-1894. Or: http://www.thechangeworks.com

Enneagram teacher Peter O'Hanrahan gives workshops on subtypes. He also writes articles for the *Enneagram Monthly* and is completing a book on subtypes. http://www.peterohanrahan.com

Enneagram teacher Katherine Chernick has also compiled a workbook on subtypes and publishes articles on her website. For information call 650-327-4404 or go to http://www.enneagram.net

The Survey Questions

Please answer the following questions:

Your age?___ sex? ___ E type? ___ wing? ___ subtype? ___

1. Of what are you aware about your type and its influence on your world view and growth path; present and past?

2. What do you wish psychotherapists or counselors would understand about your type?

3. When you are most defended, how does that look? In concrete terms, what could be or has been helpful in moving past the defense?

4. Where do therapists typically miss the best opportunity for growth in working with you?
Can you describe any negative experiences in therapy?
How did you resolve this?
How might the therapist have intervened more effectively?

5. What experiences in therapy were of benefit to you?

If you are familiar with techniques and strategies used please describe:

Why do you think these experiences and techniques were helpful to you?

7. Psychotherapists and counselors: What about your type as you experience it brings positives and negatives to the psychotherapy process?

8. If we may contact you for a follow-up interview, please give us your address or e-mail and phone.

What Therapists Said

In survey question # 7 and at our workshops, we asked therapists to assess their clinical strengths and weaknesses relative to their Enneagram styles. The results are summarized below. This is a small informal sample, but it still suggests common patterns. Note that the strengths are often the weaknesses and vice versa, depending on how they are expressed.

One Therapists:

Strengths: We are ethical about our practice, values and standards; can support a client in expressing difficult feelings and needs, even as we model our own struggle with doing the same; have compassion for difficulty, especially when the client is obviously trying to change; we work on ourselves the way we work on others; sensitive to a client's perception of criticism; when we use our instincts and are not stuck in our heads, we can be powerfully effective.

Weaknesses: We tend to impose our beliefs on others; can be judgmental; give clients answers and get attached to therapeutic outcomes; therapy can become too mental or analytical; trying to avoid the client's criticism may limit our courage to appropriately confront him; we can project our perfectionistic standards onto the client.

Two Therapists:

Strengths: We can suspend our personal needs and really focus on the client; passionate about giving, determined to help; patient about helping people warm up, we win them over; open to giving in different ways according to what the client needs; can set aside personal agendas and belief systems; very empathic and proactive.

Weaknesses: Can react with hurt feelings when clients reject what we want to give them; boundary issues, we can be overhelpful; we may come across as controlling and manipulative; come on too strong; need to be appreciated; take on too much.

Three Therapists:

Strengths: We have energy and motivation to help; goal and outcome oriented; talent for positive reframing; good at empowering; good at problem solving and finding options; we can model how to make decisions and follow them through.

Weaknesses: We may try to motivate clients by being pushy; we can be impatient; want to take over; may try to give clients answers and formulas.

Four Therapists:

Strengths: Able to empathize with clients, feel their emotions and help them identify them; can sympathize with the feeling of being misunderstood; help people identify their specialness and validate it; creative in therapy; help clients appreciate beauty in their life and integrate it; accept the client's uniqueness and reassure them that they are not flawed; flexible; can help clients be introspective and identify their own needs; communicate compassion.

Weaknesses: We can be narcissistic "navel gazers" who are unaware of a client's needs; can over-identify and get lost in a client's feelings, or have trouble separating their feelings from our own; difficulty with cognitive counseling and staying solution-focused; moving client beyond melancholy may be difficult if we are stuck in it ourselves; read too much into things – over-focus on content and meaning; get stuck in the client's pain and forget to move on.

Five Therapists:
Strengths: We can be omniscient and intuitive; keenly observant and able to listen; strong analytical and diagnostic skills; willing to research what we don't know; good boundaries; caring without being gushy or gooey; emotionally contained and dispassionate – can take intense emotion; honest and dependable; respect the client's vulnerability; can keep confidentiality; creative; can elicit a client's projections skillfully.

Weaknesses: We can be too detached and closed-off from emotions; may seem intimidating; can feed into client's push-pull patterns about intimacy; may come from head rather than heart; avoid conflict; can inhibit a client's spontaneity by example; limited energy; can feel mentally superior when defensive; elicit the client's projections accidentally; fearful under the surface.

Six Therapists:
Strengths: Able to detect bullshit and hidden agendas; intuitive; nonjudgmental – we don't jump to diagnostic conclusions or act like the expert and pronounce on your problem; excellent listeners; able to question "authority" – especially on the client's behalf; we don't foster dependency in clients.

Weaknesses: We can be self-doubting, unsure of ourselves; may be reluctant to be the "authority"; may wish to avoid conflict; can push clients into action because of our anxiety; may project our mistrust of authority onto the client's situation.

Seven Therapists:
Strengths: We have energy and humor; our creativity and reframing help clients find new ways to look at things; easy to help them brainstorm; good

at teamwork; clear boundaries; many interests; honest, we take responsibility for our actions and mistakes; resourceful and eclectic; not accepting of limits or labels; especially skilled at solution-focused brief therapy.

Weaknesses: We can be impatient with people and process; limited empathy; may avoid pain and letting experiences develop; jump to problem-solving too fast; can subtly impose our own agendas on clients; don't tolerate incompetence or a clients negative focus; can subtly impose our own agendas on the client.

Eight Therapists:

Strengths: We are energetic; seeing no limits, endless possibilities; easy to extend ego strength and be strong for others; trust our own strength; good role models for powerful lives; we work well with rebellious people, especially adolescents; supportive – and perceived so – because we acknowledge their experience of "injustice."

Weaknesses: We can be overwhelming and too confrontational; need to turn down our energy; some clients feel criticized; we can alienate fearful clients and not let them be "weak;" intolerant of some clients; impatient with chronic conditions.

Nine Therapists:

Strengths: We can offer clients unconditional support and empathy; identify easily with others. can easily see other's point of view, making us good mediators and teachers; very accepting, not much shocks us; able to participate flexibly versus having to maintain one stance; see a lot of different possibilities and solutions; understand what it means to give ourselves away and sensitive to that in others; aware of those around us; inclusive and validating.

Weaknesses: We can avoid conflict; reluctant to push clients; focus externally and tune out our instincts; not present; not having strong or healthy boundaries; procrastinating vs. doing; not saying "no;" can suffer burnout and get stubborn and rigid when exhausted; may unconsciously resent clients; fear of abandonment and disconnection can affect work with clients; difficulty prioritizing; hard to be the "expert" because we are interested in so many things; can lack boldness; may judge and inhibit our abilities with self-talk like, "I should be better," or "I'm not enough."

Carolyn Bartlett is a Licensed Clinical Social Worker with over 30 years experience in the field of mental health. Her professional work reflects a blend of secular and spiritual psychology, and she is recognized for her ability to demonstrate the applications and benefits of the Enneagram. She also designs and leads workshops on Money Psychology to help people understand their personal money history and make mindful financial choices. Carolyn has an independent psychotherapy practice in Ft. Collins, Colorado.

Articles and Information are available on the web at http://www.insightforchange.com

Index

Lightning Source UK Ltd.
Milton Keynes UK
01 July 2010
156335UK00001B/130/P